# DECISION TIME

*A Guide to the Real Answers,
Real Solutions, and Real Results
of Christ-centered Living.*

Len Stubbs

Christ-centered COACH

REAL PATH COACHING INSTITUTE

iUniverse, Inc.
New York   Bloomington

iUniverse books may be ordered through booksellers or by contacting:

iUniverse
1663 Liberty Drive
Bloomington, IN 47403
www.iuniverse.com
1-800-Authors (1-800-288-4677)

ISBN: 978-1-4401-2797-7 (sc)
ISBN: 978-1-4401-2798-4 (ebook)

Printed in the United States of America

iUniverse rev. date: 06/23/2009

*Psalm 127:1-2* -*Unless the LORD builds the house, its builders labor in vain. Unless the LORD watches over the city, the watchmen stand guard in vain. In vain you rise early and stay up late, toiling for food to eat for he grants sleep to those he loves.*

# DEDICATION

To my sons, son- in- law, and grandson I dedicate this book in hopes that you can avoid some of the mistakes and growing pains that I have failed to avoid.

To my wife, daughter, and daughter- in- laws I dedicate this book to you for without you in my life I wouldn't have been motivated to find my manhood.

In addition I dedicate this book to:

To my Christian brothers who have chosen to boldly walk on the Real Path, what a blessing it is to be invited to walk this journey with you, at my side, as my accountability partners.

To each of you that already take your Christ-centered leadership calling seriously, thank you for the example that you set in your home, in the community, in your church, and in the marketplace. You inspire me each and everyday.

To my non-Christian brothers who I thank for being open minded and curious enough to pick up and actual read this book.

From day one, it has been my aspiration to write a quality, thorough, helpful, and useful tool for all those committed to or seeking to grow in their personal relationship with the Father.

Although I have written this book for men and women alike, it is written with a focus on men putting the Father first. As such, let me set the record straight and squelch any confusion that this may create. There is no question or quarrel from this Christian that the life lessons provided to us by the walk, way, will, and word by our Father are gender neutral. In fact, we need go no further than the first book of the Bible for this truth.

In the written account of Adam's line, we are told that when God created man, he made him in the likeness of God. **In Genesis 5:2** we are instructed "He created them male and female and blessed them." In **Genesis 1:27** we are taught of mankind "So God created man in his own image, in the image of God he created him; male and female he created them."

To this end I hope, pray, and encourage both men and women to read this book, be in the word, pray fervently and seek His will in all things.

That being expressed, my caveat is that a man has written this book from the perspective of a man, and with the salvation of men and their families on my heart.

To any women who choose to pick up this book and utilize it for personal growth or to pass it on to someone significant that they really love and believe in, thank you for taking the time and making the effort to allow both yourself and those in your life to be all that they can be and all that they are called to be.

To my Father who honors and humbles me by allowing my walk to be side by side with Him, never one step ahead nor one-step behind.

**PRAYER:** As a breath prayer, Father let me slow down long enough to thank you Father for blessing me with your constant presence. You are always there for me 24/7/365. Remarkably and thankfully you are always in perfect position to allow me to lean on you when necessary and in really tough times you are both willing and positioned to completely shoulder my burden.

In conclusion, although I pray that through this book the Holy Spirit will touch the heart of all men who can then pick up the Father's calling, the Lord dedicates his life to all His Christian sons and daughters.

*In John 3:3 In reply Jesus answered, " I tell you the truth, no one can see the kingdom of God unless he is born again."*

# CONTENTS

*Matthew 7:13-14-* *"Enter through the narrow gate. For wide is the gate and broad is the road that leads to destruction, and many enter through it. But small is the gate and narrow the road that leads to life, and only a few find it.*

# FORWARD

**Martin Lifer**
**Sr. Pastor, Providence Presbyterian Church,**
**Hilton Head, South Carolina**

Jesus' teaching on our decisions and destinies includes the following:

Enter through the narrow gate. For wide is the gate and broad is the road that leads to destruction, and many enter through it. But small is the gate and narrow the road that leads to life, and only a few find it.

Therefore, everyone who hears these words of mine and puts them into practice is like a wise man who built his house on the rock. The rain came down, the streams rose, and the winds blew and beat against that house; yet it did not fall, because it had its foundation on the rock. But everyone who hears these words of mine and does not put them into practice is like a foolish man who built his house on sand. The rain came down, the streams rose, and the winds blew and beat against that house, and it fell with a great crash. [Matthew 7:13-14 and 7:24-27]

Well over a millennium before Jesus spoke those words, his Hebrew namesake, Joshua, put the key decision to his fellow Israelites.  Joshua himself chose wisely -- not only as the national leader of Israel but also as a family spiritual leader – which God calls all husbands and fathers to be:

If serving the LORD seems undesirable to you, then choose for yourselves this day whom you will serve, whether the gods your forefathers served beyond the River, or the gods of the Amorites, in whose land you are living. But as for me and my household, we will serve the LORD. [Joshua 24:15]

A man's life involves a series of decisions.  Over time, his decisions define his identity, direction, and legacy.  Even denying or avoiding hard choices is actually a decision.  The reality is that we continually live in "Decision Time."

In this book by the same name, **_Decision Time_**, Len Stubbs provides straightforward, Biblically based coaching and inspiration for men to grow up into God's Plan for their lives and life decisions.  I refer to "men," because – although the book certainly can be a great resource for everyone – (1) the particular emphasis in **_Decision Time_** is focused on men, and (2) Len's goal is to inspire those of us who are adult males to grow up into godly and effective men in all aspects of our lives.  Len draws both from biblical insights and from a personal wealth of experience and knowledge as a faithful disciple of Jesus Christ, a blessed husband and father, a successful business executive, a dedicated athlete, and an effective coach, strategist, and mentor.  The result is a comprehensive Christian life-coaching series laid out in this easy-to-read book.

Knowing Len personally as his pastor and friend, I am delighted that he has chosen to share with you in this book many of the key life-lessons God has taught Len through the years.  May God also teach, challenge, and encourage you toward a blessed and faithful Decision Time

*This book is about making the decision to place Christ first in our lives. It is about service to others. It is about finding the balance, peace, serenity, and success that can only be found by obedience to the will of the Father. It is about Causing God Joy!*

# INTRODUCTION

My personal relationship with God, my wife, my better judgment, and my continued Spirit filled journey dictates that if I am to be true to my Christ-centered manhood calling that I choose to make righteous decisions right from the get go. That reality dictated the importance that we start with the title and then continue throughout the book communicating Salt and Light in a way that was pleasing and brought honor to the Father. Hopefully, you will find that we accomplished that goal.

For the men who have decided to give this book, Christ-centered living, and successful decision making a chance I am honored to be on this journey together.

As you work your way through the text, you will become increasingly aware that the message of placing the Father first in all things is critical for a successful life.

I hope that you find the message bold and that it gets straight to the point, pulling no punches.

You have my promise that there will not be any confusion about the belief system of Decision Times' author. Toward that end let me make it perfectly clear that I am a follower of Jesus Christ. I accept forgiveness made possible only through Jesus Christ by his way, will, walk, word, life, cross, death, and resurrection. I place my full faith. trust, and confidence in Jesus Christ alone. I receive him as my Savior and Lord. I choose daily to seek his will and obediently follow and serve his calling. I acknowledge that He has always kept his promises and I ask him daily to help me keep my promise. I am bold in that truth and make no attempt to find excuses for that belief in order to be deemed politically correct.

To better understand my heart and the words of Decision Time, you might be interested to know that I hold an equally strong conviction that it is well above my grade to judge your path, walk, or decision process. These are personal decisions, which we all have to come to and live with independently. The breath of one's Christian walk is personal and has no bearing on my love or concern for the quality of his life or decision-making process.

I do, however, hold to the truth that to be truly successful in life each of us has to equip himself to make effective Christ-centered decisions.

That is in fact what we have established as a goal for this book. This book is about making the decision to place Christ first in our lives. It is about service to others. It is about finding the balance, peace, serenity, and success that can only be found by obedience to the will of the Father. It is about Causing God Joy!

This is a book that will hopefully encourage men to focus on their responsibility and take seriously the role, leadership, and accountability that the Father created men to assume.

By now you have figured out that a man who takes God at His word when he instructs us that Adam was of God and Eve of Adam has written Decision Time.

**In Genesis 2:20- 24** we are instructed that "But for Adam no suitable helper was found. So the LORD God caused the man to fall into a deep sleep; and while he was sleeping, he took one of the man's ribs and closed up the place with flesh. Then the LORD God made a woman from the rib he had taken out of the man, and he brought her to the man.

The man said, "This is now bone of my bones and flesh of my flesh; she shall be called 'woman, for she was taken out of man." For this reason, a man will leave his father and mother and be united to his wife, and they will become one flesh."

To further explain the significant of God's calling to men, lets look at Genesis 3:1-7. You will remember that the Serpent (Satan) was clever, cleverer than any wild animal God had made. He spoke to Eve: "Do I understand that God told you not to eat from any tree in the garden?"

Eve in turn responded "Not at all. We can eat from the trees in the garden. It's only about the tree in the middle of the garden that God said, 'don't eat from it; don't even touch it or you'll die.'"

The Serpent (Satan) told the Woman, "You won't die. God knows that the moment you eat from that tree, you'll see what's really going on. You'll be just like God, knowing everything, ranging all the way from good to evil."

When Eve saw that the tree looked like good eating and realized what she would get out of it, that she would know all things, she took and ate the fruit and then gave some to her husband, and he ate.

Immediately the two of them did "see what's really going on" as they saw themselves naked! They sewed fig leaves together as makeshift clothes for themselves.

It is at this point that the story of the fall of man gets interesting for Adam and all men.

Beginning in Genesis 3:8 When Adam and Eve heard the sound of God strolling in the garden in the evening breeze, they hid in the trees of the garden, hid from God, because having eaten from the tree they were now aware of their nakedness and were profoundly embarrassed.

God called to Adam: "Where are you?"

Adam responded "I heard you in the garden and I was afraid because I was naked. And I hid."

The Father all knowing was already well aware of what his son Adam had done. At this point he skillfully questions Adam, "Who told you that you were naked? Remember that neither Adam nor Eve knew of their nakedness prior to eating from the tree. God continued, "Did you eat from that tree I told you not to eat from?"

Here is where if you think about it for any amount of time, you will know in your heart of hearts the historical truth of the story of Adam and Eve.

Here is the classic alpha male defense Adam elects to make on his own behalf. Adam like all men past and present attempted to bypass all responsibility blaming it on his wife. We use the old "she made me do it" line.

Adam said, "The Woman you gave me as a companion, she gave me fruit from the tree, and, yes, I ate it."

Although there is much of importance to discuss in this story for this book, my point is that God laid responsibility at the feet of Adam for his decision to willfully disobey the command of God.

Yes, he goes on to place full responsibility for the idea on Satan as God told the serpent: "Because you've done this, you're cursed, cursed beyond all cattle and wild animals, cursed to slink on your belly and eat dirt all your life.

But the major point for man is that we are accountable for our disobedience and decision- making.

Going back to Genesis 2:23- 24 the man said, "This is now bone of my bones and flesh of my flesh; she shall be called 'woman, 'for she was taken out of man. For this reason a man will leave his father and mother and be united to his wife, and they will become one flesh."

In Proverbs 30:5 we are instructed that "Every word of God is flawless; he is a shield to those who take refuge in him." The Father said it, He meant it, and a follower of Christ I confidently and faithfully believe it.

As you prepare to jump in and get busy with this book, please, harbor no illusions that this book will be confused with any of the great literary works. You can rest assured that your head will not explode upon attempting to ascertain, check that, figure out the concepts, rationale, direction, suggestions, scripture relevancy and growth planning it contains. The good news, no check that, the great news is that the points are direct and the chapters short.

For women who may be concerned, or feeling threatened that the intent of this book is to raise up men while holding down women or that women are some how being diminished by this book…fear not. The intention of this exercise is to elevate both men and women not diminish women.

Although this book has been written with a focus on men, living a life based upon Christian principles is equally important for both men and women.

The concepts and scripture drawn upon from the Bible to improve our Christ-centered lives are gender neutral. These principles and truths allow each of us to grow closer to God's will and promise for us, which serves not only to simplify but also to improve both our thought process and lives.

This book has been written in the hopes that men will use it as a tool to focus on their Christian calling. The Bible is very clear that God instructs us that as men we have a very special calling to be the spiritual head, Christian leader, and Christ - like role model of our families.

As such, our leadership skills will be tested daily by the righteousness of the decisions we make and lives that we live. Starting with the most important decision of whether we place the Father first in our lives.

While I believe the Father when he tells us that man has a unique and substantial role in kingdom building, I also recognize the frailty of our personal constitution.

In **Hebrews 7:26-28** we are instructed that such a high priest meets our need, one who is holy, blameless, pure, set apart from sinners, exalted above the heavens. Unlike the other high priests, he does not need to offer sacrifices day after day, first for his own sins, and then for the sins of the people. He sacrificed for their sins once and for all when he offered himself.

**For the law appoints as high priests men who are weak**; but the oath, which came after the law, appointed the Son, who has been made perfect forever.

In **1 Corinthians 9:20-22** we are instructed that "To the Jews I became like a Jew, to win the Jews. To those under the law I became like one under the law (though I myself am not under the law), so as to win those under the law. To those not having the law I became like one not having the law (though I am not free from God's law but am under Christ's law), so as to win those not having the law. **To the weak I became weak, to win**

**the weak.** I have become all things to all **men** so that by all possible means I might save some."

As men, as mere humans, we are each weak. The scriptures alert us and warn us of this truth. To this end for men, surrender and obedience to the Father is both critical and frustrating. Most of us do not surrender all that well. We pretty much have control down pat but not so much with the surrender thing.

I hope that I have demonstrated that for men, the Father has carved out a very special role in his grand plan for each of us. It is that unique role and responsibility that has driven my desire to highlight the urgency of this calling and to ask men to place their relationship with our Savior top of mind at all times.

If our lives are to be fulfilling and successful, the first decision that we must come to terms with and commit ourselves to be placing the Father first. It is through this decision that we honor Him.

Honoring Him in all we do in this way offers an end result of improved focus on what is really important and it equips us with the ability to finish strong, for both kingdom building and the betterment of our families.

 As such, I hope that any women considering this book will trust me when I suggest that you can feel totally comfortable buying this for and giving it to the men in your life. If successful, this book will serve to heightening a man's commitment and selfless service to his wife, family, community, and employer.

Three suggestions that I would offer to any women buying this book for a significant male in their life is:

1) Don't bother buying this with the thought that you can read it, highlight the key points, and summarize it to your man. It doesn't work that way and that kind of defeats the

whole point of his re-claiming his responsibility and true manhood.

2) Please know that there isn't a timeline on reading and completing this journey. Finding your Christ-centered manhood isn't as easy as turning over one stone and there it is. It is a journey, that takes time, has setbacks, and victories. The man in your life will have to decide that, when, or if it is time to make changes.

The life changes which accompany putting God first that any man will have to make are changes that are often counter intuitive to everything that as men we are taught, learn, and witness in most of the role models who surround us and affect our thought processes. A personal daily relationship with the Father changes all that, as he is the perfect role model and example for us to emulate.

My hope is that this book will put all men one-step closer to this life altering decision. One step that will bring them infinitely closer to finding true success, happiness, and fulfillment. One-step closer to being all that we are called to be.

3) When giving it as a gift please be loving. Think of how you would feel if you were told that the new dress that you just purchased didn't accentuate your body type. The reality is that you are giving a man a book that deals with him finding his Christ-centeredness. You are asking him to use this book to learn how to make more Christ like decisions.

Surely you can see that this just might put him on the defensive a little. You could understand that he might think, just for a second, that you are questioning his manhood. The reality is that by giving him this book you are encouraging him to be all that he has been called to be.

That is the message that needs to be communicated.

My suggestion is that when giving it as a gift you consider something clever like asking him to give it a read and tell you what all the fuss is about because as a woman it is just a little outside your strike zone.

Let me end this introduction taking the opportunity to thank each of you who actually decide to read this book. If you have invested the time, energy, and financial resources for this book then you may be interested to know that In keeping with our calling to make Christ like decisions, always seeking His will, the first fruits of this book will be donated to Kingdom Building.

If you have enjoyed and felt equipped and blessed by this book I am going to call on you to both pass the book on and adopt a Kingdom building project, actively work on that ministry, and do your part to fund and build that ministry.

Men it is Decision Time. Whom do you decide to honor? Will it be human nature, man, you or the Creator of all things?

In Genesis 1:1- 2:4 of The Message, we are instructed that God created Heaven and Earth. We are told that First God created the Heavens and Earth. That literally means that the heavenly Father created all that we see and all that we don't see.

The picture is communicated that Earth was a soup of nothingness, a bottomless emptiness, and an inky blackness. God's Spirit brooded like a bird above the watery abyss.

God spoke: "Light!" And light appeared. God saw that light was good and separated light from dark. God named the light Day and he named the dark Night.

It was evening and then it was morning. Day One

On Day Two God spoke: "Sky! In the middle of the waters; he separated water from water!" God made the sky. He separated the water under sky from the water above sky. And there it was: he named sky the Heavens.

It was evening and then it was morning.

On Day Three God spoke: "Separate! Water-beneath-Heaven, gather into one place; Land, appear!" And there it was. God named the land Earth. He named the pooled water Ocean. God saw that it was good.

God spoke: "Earth, green up! Grow all varieties of seed-bearing plants, every sort of fruit-bearing tree." And there it was. Earth produced green seed-bearing plants, all varieties, and fruit-bearing trees of all sorts. God saw that it was good.

It was evening and then it was morning.

On Day Four God spoke: "Lights! Come out! Shine in Heaven's sky! Separate Day from Night. Marking seasons and days and years,

Lights in Heaven's sky to give light to Earth." And there it was.

God made two big lights, the larger to take charge of Day, The smaller to be in charge of Night; and he made the stars. God placed them in the heavenly sky to light up Earth and oversee Day and Night, to separate light and dark. God saw that it was good.

It was evening and then it was morning.

On Day Five God spoke: "Swarm, Ocean, with fish and all sea life! Birds, fly through the sky over Earth!" God created the huge whales, all the swarm of life in the waters, and every kind and species of flying birds. God saw that it was good. God blessed them: "Prosper! Reproduce! Fill Ocean! Birds reproduce on Earth!"

It was evening and then it was morning.

On Day Six God spoke: "Earth, generate life! Every sort and kind:

Cattle and reptiles and wild animals of all varieties." And there it was:

Wild animals of every species, Cattle of all kinds, every sort of reptile and insect. God saw that it was good.

God spoke: "Let us make human beings in our image, make them reflecting our nature so they can be responsible for the fish in the sea, the birds in the air, the cattle, And, yes, Earth itself, and every animal that moves on the face of Earth." God created human beings; he created them God -like, Reflecting God's nature.

He created them male and female. God blessed them: "Prosper! Reproduce! Fill Earth! Take charge! Be responsible for fish in the sea and birds in the air, for every living thing that moves on the face of Earth."

Then God said, "I've given you every sort of seed-bearing plant on Earth and every kind of fruit-bearing tree, given them to you for food.

To all animals and all birds, everything that moves and breathes, I give whatever grows out of the ground for food." And there it was.

God looked over everything he had made; it was so good, so very good!

It was evening and then it was morning.

On Day Six Heaven and Earth were finished, down to the last detail. By the seventh day God had finished his work.

On the seventh day he rested from all his work. God blessed the seventh day. He made it a Holy Day because on that day he rested from his work, the entire creating God had done.

This is the story of how it all started, of Heaven and Earth and when they were created.

Do you trust that all of this came from chance or that it was in fact a product of creative design?

Enjoy The Journey!

*I strive each day for the discernment to know His will and the strength to be obedient to His call to action or inaction. Inaction is a much more difficult instruction for me to follow. For the record, most days I fail miserably on this mission.*

# ABOUT THE AUTHOR

## WHO IS THIS GUY?

For all of you about to read this book and wondering who is this guy, what exactly are his qualifications to write a book about making the most important decision that we are called upon to make and achieving the real answers, real solutions, and real results of a Christ-centered life?

To each of you asking that question I say bravo you passed the first test of sound decision making. From my perspective, it is both a great question and the appropriate question for you to ask given what is about to be our journey together.

Your willingness to question my qualifications makes the statement that you know what it takes to be a man, you take your calling seriously, and that both your Christ-centered manhood and ability to render solid decisions are not far from your reach.

Yours is a question, which tells me that you and I are very much on the same page, brothers in spirit. It reflects that you don't have the spare time to waste, want me to waste your time, and that you want me as a first test to prove that you didn't waste your money on this book. Great stuff!

OK so who is Len Stubbs and under what authority can he help me make better decisions?

I am a former senior executive in the insurance industry and currently work as a certified Christ-centered coach. In addition to being a published freelance writer and author, I am the founder of Real Path Coaching and Real Path Coaching Institute.

My wife Linda and I have been married for thirty-two years, have three adult children and live on Hilton Head Island.

For more than thirty years, I have worked to build a solid reputation as a corporate executive, active listener, solid communicator, problem solver, trainer, leader, speaker, and coach.

As a certified Christ-centered Personal Life and Business coach, I am committed to you, your dreams, your goals, and your growth. I believe and am committed to the principle that there is no higher calling than to serve others as they seek out Real Answers, Real Solutions, and Real Results.

I believe that we are called to live a life of Salt and Light honoring the Father's plan and purpose for our lives.

I have worked diligently to earn a reputation as an honest, professional, and reliable Christ-centered coach, mentor, trainer, leader, friend, husband, and father.

I am a former athlete and insurance company executive who has conducted training for companies such as Autotrader, Cars.com, Union Mutual, Bankers Life, American Bankers Life, Shenandoah Life, Fort Dearborn Life, Companion Life, Blue Cross Blue Shield, CIMI, Classified Ventures, McClatchy

Newspapers, Can West, Driving.Ca. and The New York Times Regional News Group to name just several.

I am an avid runner, biker, kayaker, and sports enthusiast.

Most important to me is my relationship with my family, friends, clients and heavenly Father.

I am a husband, father, grandfather, son, son in law, brother in law, businessman, Stephen Minister, church Deacon heading up a prayer ministry and a Christ-centered life coach.

I am a follower of Jesus Christ. I am my Father's servant. I believe that His life, His word, His way, and His sacrifice are the road map, the Real Path which each of us should strive to walk.

I strive each day for the discernment to know His will and the strength to be obedient to His call to action or inaction. Inaction is a much more difficult instruction for me to follow. For the record, most days I fail miserably on this mission.

I am loving yet selfish; I have been successful but failed many times. My journey towards being the man, father, husband that I am called to be is always two steps forward and one step backward.

My heart, beliefs, tongue and action don't always work in sync. My actions can often be interpreted differently than my heart intends them to be interpreted.

I seek the will of the Father and at my core believe that His will be done are the four most important words ever written. Towards that end, on a daily basis, I seek to be strong enough to totally surrender.

However I see myself as a problem solver and thus control and being "the fixer" is an issue for me. As an admitted alpha male unfortunately I frequently don't actively live that belief. I often act as if I have control, which we all know I don't have. The truth is that I struggle with surrender virtually each and everyday.

I put my family first but often do what is best for me convincing myself and all that will listen that what is best for me is best for my family.

I start each day in prayer and petition. Unfortunately, within hours I have acted exactly the opposite of the example provided by my Father and the words that He speaks to my heart.

I guess that I am just like most of you working diligently to be the best that I can be and regularly coming up just a little short of the mark.

The good news is that it doesn't matter how many times we fail as we are forgiven and loved. What does matter is that we are in a committed personal relationship with the Father, seeking, and making progress towards our goal of rendering the decision to base our life on Christian principles that bring honor to Him, our family, and us.

My goal is that your life will benefit and blossom as a result of this book. My earnest hope is that you will both enjoy this book and pick up a little something helpful in your walk with the Father.

If that occurs, we will have both received a blessing.

*Have you ever noticed that during those periods when we feel good about ourselves, believing that all is going well in our lives, when we feel successful or at least feel on the brink of success that we seldom give the Father much thought or much credit.*

# CHAPTER ONE

## REAL SUCCESS

*"I don't measure a man's success by how high he climbs but how high he bounces when he hits bottom."*

General George S. Patton

In 1966 Eddie Floyd recorded the hit song Knock On Wood that opened "I don't want to lose you, this good thing that I got 'cause if I did I will surely lose a lot. I'd better knock (knock, knock) on wood baby."

Good song but in life real success doesn't usually happen as a result of good fortune or luck. Knocking on wood isn't considered in most circles as a solid strategic plan or decision process for success.

When we consider the meaning of success, we usually think of achievements such as money, fame, or power. However, many of the really successful people in history achieved none of these statuses.

Similarly and unfortunately, men who have professionally achieved great status, acquired great wealth, had far-reaching influence, and become famous are often complete dysfunctional failures with their families, in their private lives, and marriages.

So the questions become:

1) Is it possible to experience real success without experiencing the success of the Father's presence in our daily lives?

2) Would you be content to have success, power, wealth, but not a personal relationship with the Father and those you love?

3) Do you value a personal relationship with the Father and your family more than the greatest personal achievements you could experience in the world?

4) Have you taken the time to stop, reflect, and considered which definition of success is truly important to you?

5) Have you considered whether you would or have been tempted to choose accomplishments over your relationship with God or your loved one's?

6) Have you reflected on whether it may be that you have inadvertently chosen worldly success and reward over your personal walk with the Father and your family?

Here is what the Lord has to say about Success in His word.

(1) In **Exodus 33:16** – Then Moses said to Him " If your Presence does not go with us, do not bring us up from here."

(2) In **Isaiah 55:8-9** - "For my thoughts are not your thoughts neither are your ways my ways," declares the LORD. "As the heavens are higher than the earth, so are my ways higher than your ways and my thoughts than your thoughts."

(3) In **Psalm 14:1** –"The fool says in his heart, "There is no God." They are corrupt, their deeds are vile; there is no one who does good."

(4) In **Proverbs 27:17** – "As iron sharpens iron, so one man sharpens another."

(5) In **Romans 12:1-2** - "Therefore, I urge you, brothers, in view of God's mercy, to offer your bodies as living sacrifices, holy and pleasing to God—this is your spiritual act of worship. Do not conform any longer to the pattern of this world, but be transformed by the renewing of your mind. Then you will be able to test and approve what God's will is—his good, pleasing and perfect will."

(6) In **Jeremiah 17:9-10** - "The heart is deceitful above all things and beyond cure. Who can understand it? "I the LORD search the heart and examine the mind, to reward a man according to his conduct, according to what his deeds deserve."

(7) In **Mark 4:20** -" Others, like seed sown on good soil, hear the word, accept it, and produce a crop—thirty, sixty or even a hundred times what was sown."

(8) In **Mark 4:19** -" but the worries of this life, the deceitfulness of wealth and the desires for other things come in and choke the word, making it unfruitful."

(9) In 1 **Samuel 16:7**- "But the LORD said to Samuel, "Do not consider his appearance or his height, for I have rejected him. The LORD does not look at the things man looks at. Man looks at the outward appearance, but the LORD looks at the heart."

**Here are Eight (8) tips to Real Success:**

1. **Get a Knowledge and Experience Base** – Invest in yourself and your success. Get the facts, study them, call upon your skill set and experience, and if needed seek the coaching of someone knowledgeable in the area.

2. **Invest Time, Be Patient** - Success rarely comes overnight.

3. **Work Collaboratively-** Networking and bringing different perspectives and experience together with a common purpose reaps dividends.

4. **Practice Christ-centeredness** - Place your faith in the center of your life, your beliefs, and your actions.

5. **Surrender Completely** - Love your Father and trust Him without reservation.

6. **Serve Your neighbor** - Servant hood demonstrates the truth of God's unfailing love to those who feel, experience, and witness it.

7. **Commit Totally, Go For It** – You can't be a part time disciple and please your maker. Cause God Joy. Heed the words of Isaiah, "Here am I. Send me!" Run to success with all the energy you possess.

8. **Follow Faithfully** – Faith keeps us in a trusting relationship with God. Nothing is more secure or certain than that which we entrust to God. Faithfulness will stablize your decision process and move you towards success.

Have you ever noticed that during those periods when we feel good about ourselves, believing that all is going well in our lives, when we feel successful or at least feel on the brink of success that we seldom give the Father much thought or much credit. It is an unfortunate twist of fate that short-term worldly success often makes it less likely that we will take the time to either be thankful to or dependant upon the Lord.

Then the inevitable happens, we suffer a set back, reality sinks in and we once again seek out the assistance and blessing of the Father.

Paradoxically we replay and recycle this situation over and over again during our lifetime. These faux short- term successes don't last long because as the Bible teaches us they are built upon a foundation of sand not rock. Building success on a foundation of sand will most often put your long-term successes in long-term jeopardy.

When evaluating whether or not these short-term successes can hold up against the test of time, simply keep a watchful eye out to see what happens to those successes when the first storm hits.

If the successes are built on a foundation of rock, which has the Father as its center and as it's main ingredient, they will be strong enough to weather any size storm.

Remember as much as we might wish it to be otherwise, there really aren't any short cuts to real success. Real success lasts because it is based upon His plan for His truth, His plan, and His purpose for our lives.

### Six (6) Questions to Success:

1. Do you feel, overall, that your view and outlook of life is: a) Very broad, b) Average, or c) Narrow?

Why do you feel that way?

2. How frequently do you consciously, mentally step back, reflect upon, and look at the overall picture of yourself and the world around you?

3. Write a statement of what you consider real success to be. Be specific include family, work, personal time, and lifestyle. What one or two actions can you take to attain this vision?

4. What one or two actions do you take to get above the "noise level," and gain a broader perspective of and focus on Real Success?

5. What one thing, more than anything else, causes you to become shortsighted as you evaluate your long-term success goals? Do your short and long-term goals align with each other?

6. If you could write a goal that would help you keep a better or broader perspective and focus every day, what would you write?

So in the end it seems apparent that real success results from seeking the Father's will and obediently following His way, word, and walk.

In this regard, true success can only be found in the search for and the achievement of the purposes for which God created us. That is ultimately what will make us happy and insure our thirst and quest for real success.

As a final thought on this subject, interestingly earlier today, I was with some Brothers who had just returned from an incredible journey to the Holy Land. Oddly enough the subject of knocking on wood came up. It seems that on their trip they happened upon the origins of the old saying when wishing luck, success, and prosperity of "knock on wood". It appears that the saying originated because following the crucifixion and resurrection of Christ, Christians who needed miracles would go to the spot where Christ's cross was kept and would touch the cross.

Given its beginnings that I guess that knocking on wood is a pretty solid strategic plan. Apparently based upon its origin knocking on wood is an act of faith not luck. Go figure.

If you want to find **Real Success** ask yourself the questions. In whose life did I make a difference today? Am I living a life that surrenders to my Father's will? What is my foundation built upon? In fact reflect upon these questions many times each day.

**PRACTICE:** To practice your perspective of success this week, I'd like you to start each morning by asking yourself two questions: 1. "How is my perspective today?" 2. "What can I do today to see the world, and my life in it, in the broadest possible perspective regarding Real Success?" (Be sure to write your thoughts and ideas on "building your perspective," in your Success Journal.)

**PRAYER:** Heavenly Father all honor, praise and glory to you. Thank you for the many blessings that you have chosen to provide in my life. Father what an honor it is to know that you wait patiently each day for our time together. I come to you at this point seeking discernment as to your will for my life.

I know that when I align my life to your will that my life will be blessed with success. Thank you Father for being here for me. I love you Lord.

*Each and everyday literally thousands of people make a conscious decision, a practice, and a career of putting others ahead of themselves by following a higher calling of salt and light. By follow a higher calling of service making a decision and commitment to put others in and around their lives first.*

# CHAPTER TWO

## PUTTING OTHERS FIRST

"Be gentle and you can be bold; be frugal and you can be liberal; avoid putting yourself before others and you can become a leader among men. "

Lao Tzu

**Up next our top stories:**

**"Unknown man stops assailant wants no credit".**

**"Firefighters Fight back Flames to Save Family" News at 11.**

**"Hundreds of Christian volunteers rebuild homes destroyed in flood."**

When everyday citizens like you and me perform extraordinary feats of courage, when the average Joe puts his self-interest and safety second and places the interest of others first, when we witness Christ- centeredness rather than self-centeredness demonstrated we pay attention. When we hear and see these acts of neighborly, Christian love, we immediately and reflexively sit up, and take notice.

These types of acts of goodwill, service to others, and brotherly love grab our attention. These selfless acts motivate us to reflect on the condition of our heart, inspire us to change, give us hope, and motivate us to act on our best instincts.

But beyond the headlines, the commentators, the cameras and hidden from the sight of most of our daily lives are other individuals, again like each of you, who also motivate us to do God sized tasks and inspire hope. Each and everyday literally thousands of people make a conscious decision, a practice, and a career of putting others ahead of themselves by following a higher calling of salt and light. By follow a higher calling of service making a decision and commitment to put others in and around their lives first.

These individuals, each a role model, each a hero, and each making a conscious decision to follow the example set by our savior Jesus Christ himself who "made himself nothing, taking the very nature of the servant." **Philippians 2:7**

In one of the most electric passages in the Bible (**Philippians 2 1-11**) Paul describes the real path that Jesus elected to walk for all his children. A journey which took him from the glory of heaven, to death on a cross, and ascension back again to heaven sitting at the right hand of the Father.

There can be no debate that Jesus made the ultimate sacrifice to save us from our sins. Paul says that even though Jesus was God, he gave up his heavenly status to save a rebellious and sinful human population. He shed His blood so that we might receive forgiveness.

Each of us as Christians are called to via our actions and lives to boldly show ourselves as followers of Jesus. We are each called to put the interest of others above our own. To "Love the Lord your God with all your heart and with all your soul and with all your strength and with all your mind; and, 'Love your neighbor as yourself." (**Luke 10:27**)

While such sacrifice is counter intuitive and may be difficult at times, I think we can all agree that no amount of human difficulty could ever or will ever rival the sacrifice Jesus knowingly, lovingly, and willingly made for us that day at Calvary.

Following his way, his word, and his example will take on different shapes and forms for each of us.

It could be as simple as deciding not to park in a handicap parking spot for a quick trip into a store, giving up a prime parking space to an elderly couple, giving your seat up on mass transportation or as difficult as giving up a lucrative career to follow Jesus' call to a ministry or Para ministry position.

**Here is what the Lord has to say about Putting Others First in His word.**

(1) In **1 Corinthians 10:24** –" Nobody should seek his own good, but the good of others. "

(2) In **Mark 10: 45** - "For even the Son of Man did not come to be served, but to serve, and to give His life as a ransom for many"

(3) In **Luke 23:34** - Jesus said, "Father, forgive them, for they do not know what they are doing."

(4) In **Philippians 2:6-8** - "Your attitude should be the same as that of Christ Jesus: Who, being in very nature God, did not consider equality with God something to be grasped, but made Himself nothing, taking the very nature of a servant, being made in human likeness. And being found in appearance as a man, He humbled Himself and became obedient to death— even death on a cross!"

(5) In **1 Corinthians 8:13** – "Therefore, if what I eat causes my brother to fall into sin, I will never eat meat again, so that I will not cause him to fall."

So in the end, how exactly do you plan your life so that your focus is to put others first? **Here are Four (4) tips that I think you may find helpful.**

## Four (4) Tips to Putting Others First

1. **Prepare Your Heart** – God created you with unique gifts, ideas, and passions, and longs for you to connect with His redemptive purpose. The path of discovering God's purpose for your life starts with the practice of putting others first as it requires surrender and humility.

2. **Let Go** - Consciously commit to moving from self-centeredness to Christ-centeredness.

3. **Follow His Lead** – Jesus took on the lowest of lowly slave duties… that of a foot washer. Do you need a better example of servant hood?

4. **Sharpen Your Focus On Jesus** - Seek a constant personal relationship with your heavenly Father. With committed, trusting friends, associates, accountability partners and family at our sides, learn how to be free from selfishness and find liberation, and growth from the practice of putting others first.

Each of us is called to live out Paul's call to servant hood. We need to continually "consider others better than ourselves " as a part of a life that is devoted to Jesus Christ, who did after all provide us with the ultimate example of selflessness and servant hood.

This adjustment to a life of service is without question a difficult decision to make as it requires us to reduce to time, energy, and resources spent on our desires, wishes, and wants. However the reward for the willingness to make this decision is great. The reality is that loving and caring for the needs of others is the highest calling that we can endeavor.

Clearly we are not all blessed to be in a position to decide to put a stop to our lives in order that we might serve others full time. That in fact may not be the purpose that the Father has for our lives. The truth often is that financial realities, family obligations, time requirements, and a host of other issues make that decision impossible. The point to be made here is this is not an all or nothing proposition.

You don't have to make the difficult decision to sacrifice it all, you only have to decide to put others first in the life you are currently living. That decision in itself will change your life beyond belief.

**Six (6) Questions To Help Put Others First:**

1. Rate the level of respect and courtesy that you typically show for the attitudes, position, achievements, experience, and qualities of the people that you come in contact with. Rate yourself 1 to 10, with 1 being someone who exhibits a high level of putting others first, and 10 being the lowest level of putting first others. Why?

2. In general, do you typically show respect for the other person when you do not agree with their point of view? How do you show it?   (Example: "I respect your point of view, but I don't agree with you.")

3. Think of one person you know, who is always putting others first. What does that person do that makes them stand out?

4. To what extent do you let your own opinions, beliefs or needs stop you from putting others first?

5. Overall, are you completely satisfied with the level of respect and concern, which you show to other people in every situation?

6. Is there anything you would like to do, or practice, that would help other people see you as someone who puts others first? (Note: We almost always respect the people most, who respect others most.)

As a final thought on this subject, Christ-centeredness clearly causes God joy. As such consider continually making decisions and seek to grow closer to Christ. Always decide to continue to seek to grow as a person, pushing you to more fully to reflect Christ in words, deeds, and actions.

Please don't misinterpret I am certainly not recommending that each of us should give away all our possessions and live homeless. I am however suggesting that as " Jesus said to them all: "If anyone would come after me, he must deny himself and take up his cross daily and follow me. For whoever wants to save his life will lose it, but whoever loses his life for me will save it. What good is it for a man to gain the whole world, and yet lose or forfeit his very self? I am saying keep putting others first top of mind.

I hope that you will make and take some time to read Philippians 2 again, slowly, methodically, each time absorbing the loving, amazing nature and example of Jesus' selfless sacrifice.

**PRACTICE:** To practice the concept of Putting Others First this week, I'd like you to consciously observe how you treat everyone you meet throughout the week. At the end of each day, rate yourself on how well you did that day, and write the details and your scores down in your Success Journal. If you find any behavior of yours that you think needs fixing, write it down, and decide what to do about it.

**PRAYER:** Heavenly Father all honor, praise and glory to you. Thank you for the many blessings that you have chosen to provide in my life. Father In **Mark 10: 45** you teach us that **"For even the Son of Man did not come to be served, but to serve, and to give His life as a ransom for many"** Thank you Lord for providing us with such a vivid example of the importance of putting others first in our lives. I come to you seeking the strength of Christ-centeredness for my life. I know the importance of aligning my life to your life. Bless me with the strength to live by your example Thank you Father for being here for me. I love you Lord.

*Christians do not forget the past; instead they learn valuable lessons not to repeat from the past. But on the other hand, because of their personal relationship with God, they do not allow themselves to be controlled or motivated by their past. For Christians their past is forgotten and has been paid for by the blood of our savior. Christians always strive to acknowledge and take responsibility for their own present day actions. Christians look to the future with hope, dreams, and aspirations.*

# CHAPTER THREE

## LOOKING FORWARD

**"Change is the law of life. And those who look only to the past or present are certain to miss the future."**

**-John F. Kennedy, former U.S. President**

How many of us on occasion, upon reflection, find ourselves trapped looking to our past as opposed to looking to our future? How many of us find safety living in the glory of past accomplishments as opposed to looking forward to our next great achievement? How many of us if we were being honest would have to admit that we find it comfortable reflecting on the past in order that we might avoid the challenges and uncertainty of the future?

Secular society constantly affirms, sells, and wants us to accept a false premise that the overriding influence in our life and in our future is our past.

We are taught that it is acceptable and understandable to make a habit of using excuses and blaming others for our failures. We are all victims of our past. If you came from a difficult home life and your current life is a mess, it was obviously and without doubt the earlier time (past) that determined the negative direction of your life today. If your culture was treated unfairly somewhere in the past any future failure in your life can be written off as a direct result of that unfair, unjust, and unforgivable past treatment. If you were hurt, abused or if your youth was spent in rebellion, it is understandable if the remainder of your life is spent struggling with your past.

The result of all this preoccupation with the past is that at times we feel so worn out, beat up, and stressed out that we are not certain if we can take another step forward.

Heck, we aren't even certain whether of not it is worth the effort to get out of bed in the morning. I think that it is fair to conclude that the world is preoccupied with the past because it is weary of its future.

The world has decided to choose victimization over self-responsibility. The world would have us believe that we aren't responsible victims of our past decisions, which would be a reasonable argument, but instead that we are victims of our past experiences.  The world is preoccupied with the past because it has chosen to face an uncertain future.

Christians on the other hand, live in freedom because through Calvary and the New Covenant, Christ overcame our past. The "old things" have been done away with and "new things" have come (**2 Cor. 5:17**). God has so totally forgiven the Christians sin that He chooses not to remember it (**Isa.43: 25**).

Don't misunderstand my point; Christians do not forget the past, instead they learn valuable lessons not to repeat from the past.

But on the other hand because of their personal relationship with God, they do not allow themselves to be controlled or motivated by their past. For Christians, their past is forgotten and has been paid for by the blood of our savior. Christians always strive to acknowledge and take responsibility for their own present day actions. Christians look to the future with hope, dreams, and aspirations.

**Here is what the Lord has to say about Looking Forward in His word.**

(1) In **Philippians 3:13** – "No, dear brothers and sisters, I have not yet achieved it, but I focus on this one thing: Forgetting the past and looking forward to what lies ahead."

(2) In **Ephesians 5:15-17**- "Be very careful, then, how you live—not as unwise but as wise, making the most of every opportunity, because the days are evil. Therefore do not be foolish, but understand what the Lord's will is."

(3) In **Isaiah 40:31**- "but those who trust in the Lord will find new strength. They will soar high on wings like Eagles. They will run and not grow weary. They will walk and not faint."

(4) In **Philippians 2:14-16** –" Do all things without grumbling or questioning, that you may be blameless and innocent, children of God without blemish in the midst of a crooked and twisted generation, among whom you shine as lights in the world, holding fast to the word of life, so that in the day of Christ I may be proud that I did not run in vain or labor in vain."

(5) In **Romans 8:28** – "And we know that God causes all things to work together for good to those who love God, to those who are called according to His purpose."

You may be in a place in your life where making a decision to look forward just doesn't seem very practical. It could be that your world seems to be imploding in front of your very eyes. Times may be on a slippery slope down hill. You may be experiencing a personal loss, out of work, financial disaster, legal issues, a tragedy in your family life, or any number of other nightmares that may have you so preoccupied with them that looking forward is just impossible. If this is the circumstances that you or someone you know find yourself in, then believe it or not this chapter is really for you.

If this is your current lot in life, remember that patience is a virtue. Be patient with God, hang in there, and forgetting your past, push on looking forward. Remember that Jesus overcame death on a cross and that He is bigger than all our problems. His word is flawless and He promises us a loving future.

With that truth and promise in mind, decide to trust Him and look forward. His has a great success story in your future.

So in the end, the question becomes how exactly do you plan your life so that your focus is to always look forward and live in the present?

**Here are Five (5) tips that I think you may find helpful.**

**Five (5) tips to Look Forward:**

**1. PUT GOD FIRST-** Christ must be at the center of everything. The Bible teaches us that our one and only priority is to keep Him, His Kingdom, and His righteousness first in everything. His will and our service to Him is our priority.

**2. Focus on the Goal** – By definition, goals are ahead of us and are to be attained. Focus on the present, push forward and both success and happiness will be yours.

**3. Let it Go** - Move from the past and on to the future. The reality is that if we make a habit of using excuses and blaming others for our failures we will never reach a point of responsibility, liberation, and growth.

**4. New Strength-** God's purpose for our lives requires a power beyond our human capabilities. Our Lord promises to renew our strength and enable us to enjoy the abundant life He intends for each of us.

**5. Sharpen Your Focus On Jesus** – Seek a constant personal relationship with your heavenly Father. With committed, trusting friends, associates, accountability partners and family at our sides, learn how to be free from the past, handle the day-to-day pressures in the present and move forward to the future God has planned.

**Six Questions to Looking Forward:**

1. To what extent do you believe that your life now, is affected in any negative way, from things that happened to you in the past? a) Almost never, b) Occasionally, c) Frequently. Why? What are those experiences?

2. Do you make a determined effort to look forward and let past negatives go? What do you do about any negatives that could still be holding you back?

3. What do you think when you meet or know someone who allows their past to hurt their present?

4. Do you ever see past problems or failures as adequate reasons why you should not succeed now?

5. What one negative from your past, if any, would you most like to get past, and move beyond it? (Note: Offer no personal "therapy" or "psychological counseling" on your part when you discuss this.)

6. If you were to write a goal, to get past any problems from the past, what would you say? Secular society tends to focus on the grief and experiences that they are overcoming. Christians tend to look forward focusing on not what they have been but instead on what they are becoming. Christians know that the Holy Spirit is alive and working to transform them into the image of Christ. Christians know that eventually each and every injustice that may come their way will be addressed and every hurt healed.

The Christian's future is so full, rich and exciting that it absolutely overwhelms whatever may have happened in the past.

If you are falling into the trap of being preoccupied with your past, ask God to open your eyes to the incredible future that awaits you and continually look forward to that purpose that the Lord has planned for your life.

As a final thought on this subject, I would suggest that you continually seek to grow closer to Christ, always seek to continue growing as a person, pushing yourselves to more fully reflect Christ in all words, deeds, and actions. The point here is not that we should forget our past, but rather that we should not dwell in it. Living in the past inevitably means that we stop growing and learning. For success and happiness, make the decision to look forward.

**PRACTICE:** To practice the concept of letting go of the past this week, I'd like you to find three creative, positive ways for you to reward yourself for making the choice to live in the present. Write down the three areas you have selected and work on them diligently.

**PRAYER:** Heavenly Father all honor, praise and glory to you. Thank you for the many blessings that you have chosen to provide in my life. Father In **Philippians 3:13** Paul reminds us that **"No, dear brothers and sisters, I have not yet achieved it, but I focus on this one thing: Forgetting the past and looking forward to what lies ahead."** Thank you Lord for providing us with words, which place our focus and attention squarely on the future that you have planned for us. We look forward to fulfilling your promise for our future. I accept the importance of surrendering control of my future and looking forward to you and you only. Bless me with the faith needed to live by your example. Thank you Father for being here for me. I love you Lord.

*The Bible is clear that anyone who cannot communicate will not lead well, long or successfully. It should be fairly obvious that effective communication involves more than just speaking and hearing. Real communication can only take place when both parties move beyond speaking and hearing to actual understanding.*

# CHAPTER FOUR

## ACTIVE AND EFFECTIVE LISTENING

**"The greatest motivational act one person can do for another is to listen."**

**Roy E. Moody**

Since you have chosen to take the time to read this chapter, rather than simply skip over it, can we right out of the starting blocks stipulate and agree that one of the keys to establishing long term, solid, and successful relationships is effective communication? Can we also agree that for effective communication to occur, there must be active listening? Lastly can we agree that in order to be an active and effective listener we must make the decision to focus on the needs, actions, and words of others verses what we have to say on each and every subject?

Active listening requires the development of three personal qualities in the listener: Desire, commitment, and patience.

**Here is what the Lord has to say about listening in His word.**

(1)    In the New Testament, the Lord warns us to consider carefully what you hear (**Mark 4:24)** and how you hear (**Luke 8:18**).

(2)    In **Mark 4:9** the Lord warned, "Whoever has ears to hear had better listen!" and again in verse 23 He said "If anyone has ears to hear, he had better listen!

(3) Seven times, once in each of the letters to the seven churches in **Revelation 2 and 3** we read, "He who has an ear let him hear what the Spirit says to the churches."

(4) In **Proverbs 18:13** it is written, "Spouting off before listening to the facts is both shameful and foolish."

(5) In **Proverbs 18:2** Solomon offers a direct open evaluation of those who would rather talk than listen: "A fool finds no pleasure in understanding but delights in airing his own opinions".

(6) In **Deuteronomy 18:15** Moses wrote "The Lord your God will raise up for you a prophet like me from among you—from your fellow Israelites; you must listen to him."

(7) In **James 1:19-20**- "My dear brothers, take note of this: Everyone should be quick to listen, slow to speak and slow to become angry, for man's anger does not bring about the righteous life that God desires"

(8) In **1 Samuel 3:10**-The LORD came and stood there, calling as at the other times, "Samuel! Samuel!" Then Samuel said, "Speak, for your servant is listening."

The Bible is clear that anyone who cannot communicate will not lead well, long or successfully. It should be fairly obvious that effective communication involves more than just speaking and hearing. Real communication can only take place when both parties move beyond speaking and hearing to actual understanding.

Most of us spend vast amounts of time, energy and resources developing other foundation skills, such as long-term planning, time management and public speaking. All of which are unquestionably very important in our quest for self-improvement and success. But at a minimum, it is at least equally important to make the commitment to prioritize your time and effort to developing the skill of listening.

This is a critical skill for long term success, so to any and all who truly desire and strive to be successful, I recommend that you waste no time coming to the decision to make whatever investment necessary to master this skill set.

**An easy Six (6)-step process is:**

(1) **Attention:** Listen without interruption, debate, or judgment

(2) **Consideration:** Listen to what they are saying, listen for what they are not saying, listen for what they are thinking while they are talking.

(3) **Body Language:** Give your complete attention and focus to not only words but to the physical reactions to those with whom you are communicating.

(4) **Reflection:** When they have finished speaking, reflect back to them what you heard them say

(5) **Respect:** Effective listening is a matter of respect; do you respect the person communicating with you? If so, show them the consideration and courtesy to respect their time and words. Listen intently.

(6) **Discipline:** The discipline of stillness is a critical skill to master and place into action if you are to be a truly effective listener.

Proverbs 13 teaches us the truth about communication: "He who answers before listening – that is his folly and his shame."

Most great communicators readily acknowledge that active listening is the number one communication skill required for success. Effective communication involves more than just speaking and hearing.

Real communication only takes place when both parties move beyond speaking and hearing to a clear understanding of intention, desire, needs, goals, aspirations and desired end result.

**Six (6) Questions to Effective Listening:**

1. How would you rate your listening skills: a) Very high b) Average c) Low.  Why did you give yourself that rating?

2. How often do you consciously think about listening actively? In what situations?

3. Do you ever interrupt when you should not? In what situations do you do that?  (Do you have a habit of interrupting or a habit of listening?)

4. In general, what is your opinion of people who you notice to be active listeners? (Also, why do you feel that way about them?)

5. When you listen, do you lean forward, look directly at the person talking, or show in your face that you're actively interested in what they have to say? (What is your typical body language saying when someone else is talking?)

6. If you wanted to improve your listening skills, what is one thing you will do, starting now, that would help you?

When we think about and consider the importance of listening, think about the Isaiah who proclaims the importance of listening saying "He wakes me up in the morning, Wakes me up, and opens my ears to listen as one ready to take orders. The Master, God, opened my ears, and I didn't go back to sleep, didn't pull the covers back over my head." The Bible has countless examples citing the power and effectiveness of listening. The Father challenges us to become effective, active, reactionary listeners.

**PRACTICE:** To practice this skill of listening over the course of the next seven days take the time and make the commitment to really listen to everyone who's talking to you. Listen to what they are saying, listen for what they are not saying, and listen for what they are thinking while they are talking. At the same time, make certain that you let your body language show that you are listening. Practice this even while you are on your mobile. Then in your Success Journal, place a note at the top of the page to practice your active /effective listening skills for each of the next 21 days. Twenty - one (21) consecutive days creates a new skill. Decide today to invest in yourself for success.

**PRAYER:** Heavenly Father all honor, praise and glory to you. Thank you for the many blessings that you have chosen to provide in my life. Father In **1 Samuel 3:9 Eli** instructed

Samuel to respond to you "**So Eli told Samuel, "Go and lie down, and if he calls you, say, 'Speak, LORD, for your servant is listening.' " So Samuel went and lay down in his place.**" Thank you Lord for providing us with wisdom that teaches us to take whatever time is necessary to listen for your words of instruction for our lives. I patiently wait for you to reveal your heart to me. Bless me with the patience and skill needed to wait and listen for your voice. Thank you Father for being here for me. I love you Lord

*The Bible provides us with a firm plan on how to establish and set goals. To no surprise God clearly articulates principles in Scripture for setting and reaching goals.*

# CHAPTER FIVE

## GOALS AND GOAL SETTING

**"Deciding to commit yourself to long term results, rather than short term fixes, is as important as any decision you'll make in your lifetime."**

**Tony Robbins**

I admit it; I spent half of this past weekend watching a Rocky movie marathon. The six movie series first hit the screens in 1976 entitled Rocky and it ended; at least I think that it has ended, with the sixth and final segment Rocky Balboa released in 2006. The Rocky series, which admittedly will not be confused with any of the great all time cinema masterpieces, are totally American in theme. To that end, they provide instructive examples to the importance of making solid long-term decisions in the area of goals and goal setting.

The story line tells a rags-to-riches American Dream story of Rocky Balboa, an uneducated, kind-hearted and tenacious club fighter who gets a shot at the world heavyweight championship when Apollo Creed the champ decides that America is the land of opportunity and wants to give a nobody from Philly a shot at the title.

Interestingly, each of these six movies makes some fairly profound statements on goals, goal setting, leadership, humility and fleeting success vs. real success.

In the Rocky series, we learn that the goal of winning can involve several different outcomes. For most of us, when we set a goal of winning, our end goal would be to become champion of the boxing world.

This is, of course, a goal that if attained could quickly be lost the very next fight. This is a goal without a soul. This is really an outcome as opposed to a goal.

On the other hand, Rocky's goal and definition of winning is insightful and instructional. He lays that goal out to Adrian the night before the fight. His goal is to compete, to give his best effort, and continue to fight until the final bell. His goal is one of character building, loving the battle and lifetime building blocks vs. just an end result.

In Rocky Balboa (2006), he completes this circle as he provides his son the ultimate life lesson on goals and goal setting. Reaching for a long-term life goal that has staying power, Rocky recants that: life isn't about how hard you can land on it but is about how hard a punch you can take and still get back up fighting. This is the goal he had for both his life and his son's life. This is a goal with a long-term lifespan.

Goal setting is an important skill to learn and develop. The decisions to take and the actions necessary to be more successful in life, require the decision to improve your goal setting skills.

Most highly successful people are consciously and consistently goal oriented. They set immediate, short term and long-term goals that align with each other. They understand the importance of goal setting and set aside the time to consider, decide upon, and establish goals and the plans to attain them.

More importantly they take the time and make the effort to actually go through the exercise of writing down their goal and plan for attaining it so that they can see it, feel it, be reminded of it on a regular basis and evaluate it.

The Bible provides us with a firm plan on how to establish and set goals. To no surprise God clearly articulates principles in Scripture for setting and reaching goals.

**Here is what the Lord has to say about Goal Setting in His word.**

(1) In **Proverbs 11:27**- For one, he says you'll be respected if you set good goals.

(2) In **Proverbs 16:9** - "We should make plans, counting on God to direct us."

(3) In **Proverbs 24:3**-"Any enterprise is built by wise planning, becomes strong through common sense, and profits wonderfully by keeping abreast of the facts."

(4) In **Proverbs 13:16**-"A wise man thinks ahead, a fool doesn't and even brags about it."

(5) In **James 4:13-15**- "Now listen, you who say, "Today or tomorrow we will go to this or that city, spend a year there, carry on business and make money." Why, you do not even know what will happen tomorrow. What is your life? You are a mist that appears for a little while and then vanishes. Instead, you ought to say, "If it is the Lord's will, we will live and do this or that."

Diana Scharf Hunt once wrote, " Goals are dreams with deadlines." I would add to that statement that goals not written down and dated for completion are nothing more than wishes.

As you take ownership of your goals and goal setting, what type of changes to your life are you considering? Are you interested in setting goals in the area of personal development, financial freedom, weight loss, recreational opportunities, exercise, employment status, or family focus? The list of goals that we choose to reach for could include any of these and a long list of other possibilities. My question for you to consider is before deciding to set a specific goal(s) have you spent anytime with the Father seeking the direction that He would like to see you grow in. Consider just for a second which goals the Father would most want you to set that would put you on pace to attain His plan and purpose for your life. All too often we elect to make decisions after which we expect the Lord to bless them. Our calling is to seek His will and adjust our lives and goals accordingly.

If in the past you have controlled and set your goals, take a moment and reflect upon your success level attaining these goals. If you find that you have experienced less success than you would have anticipated, perhaps the reason for your low hit percentage is that by yourself you simply do not have the strength, will, focus, power or commitment to reach your desired goal.

If this possibility resonates at all with you I would suggest that you consider consulting with the Lord prior to establishing and setting your goals. If you and He are on the same page God himself will energize and sustain your efforts to successfully complete your goal.

The Father is at all times working to provide us the strength, focus, and power to improve our lot. It sure is nice to have an accountability partner whose name is above all others, whose name is a mighty tower, whose name promises to save us if we just decide to run to it.

**Here are eight (8) tips to successful Goal Setting.**

**Eight Rules of Goal Setting**

1) Goal setting is a skill. You can learn a skill so each of us can master and benefit from goal setting.

2) All goals must be written down and measured. A goal not written down is nothing more than a wish.

3) All goals must be attainable. Being able to reach them is important, so goals need to be reasonable and reachable.

4) All goals must be specific. The optimum way to know if we have arrived at our goals is to be as specific as possible.

5) All goals must be Personal. Unless we own them we are unlikely to pursue them.

6) All goals should begin with the word to. The word is a call to action. Goals are a call to action

7) All goals must be dated. Dates give us a measuring point and the opportunity to evaluate our process and progress.

8) A goal plan always includes obstacles and action plans. In fact, action steps are in fact more important than the goal itself

As we begin to make real progress in this area and successfully accomplish goals, we often forget to take the time to be thankful and appreciative for that success. It is all too much a part of human nature to move on to the next goal without even so much as a mental check in the box acknowledging our victory.

At the root of the Christian experience is thankfulness and appreciation for each of life's blessings. As a Christian, you should be comfortable looking beyond the success to its source. God waits on our response to victories. He deserves our thanks, worship and praise. You deserve to enjoy your victory, you worked diligently to attain it so take the time to celebrate victories with the Father.

## Six (6) Questions To Goal Setting:

1) How frequently do you set goals, how much time do you spend considering them and what kind of goals do you usually set?

2) Are your goals usually long term (more than a year away) or short-term goals (daily, weekly, and monthly goals)?

   Give me two or three examples of goals you have set up until now. Do your long and short-term goals align with each other?

3. How do you determine which goals you set?

4. How do you typically track and monitor your progress on the goals you set?

5. What do you do, typically, when you have set a goal, and do not reach it?

6. Do you believe you are willing to make the decision to faithfully set, track, and monitor goals in the key areas of your life? Why?

So in the end, goal setting is an important, serious, in fact critical skill to develop and utilize. Equally as important as goal setting, we need to be careful and aware that we are not so inflexible and anxious about life that we make rigid plans, which prevent us from successfully attaining our goals.

While flexibility is our key to successfully attaining our goals, we should also take great care not to be so uninspired as to make no plans at all. Rather, with all humility, let us submit our plans to the Lord, and work for his glory, while we retain the flexibility to adjust to His direction.

Make the decision to put God first in your life and top of mind if you truly want to achieve a level of goal setting, which is world class, consistent and successful. Christ must be at the center of everything. The Bible teaches us that our one and only priority is to keep Him, His Kingdom, and His righteousness first in everything. His will and our service to Him should always be our priority.

Decide today to more fully develop this skill. A decision to reaching real growth in this area will heighten your long-term chances for success.

**PRACTICE:** To practice the concept of Goal Setting this week, I'd like you to make a "dream list" of literally everything you'd like to be, have, or change in your life. (Plan to take some time for you to do this.) Take the limits off. Let your imagination wander. Write down anything and everything. Write the longest list you can – both short term and long-term goals. Then prioritize them, making certain that the long-term and short-term goals line up to the same end result.

**PRAYER:** Heavenly Father all honor, praise and glory to you. Thank you for the many blessings that you have chosen to provide in my life. Father in **Proverbs 11:27** you guide us that **"For one, he says you'll be respected if you set good goals,"** I come to you seeking knowledge and skill in the area of goal setting. More importantly, I seek to only chase goals that are of your will and direction. Help me to see where your will is at work. Thank you Father for being here for me. I love you Lord.

*I am speaking specifically about time where you do nothing except listen. You may be asking yourself listen to what? I am suggesting that you manage this portion of your time to listen for something. Something that you couldn't possible hear above the clutter of your own voice. Something so amazing that it may alter your life and your decision path for all eternity. Is that worth allocating time to?*

# CHAPTER SIX

## TIME MANAGEMENT

**"Money, I can only gain or lose. But time I can only lose. So, I must spend it carefully."**

**Author Unknown**

Time is our great adversary. Time is a commodity of which we are continually running short. The amount of total time available to us is out of our control. Time is a fixed asset. Time is a valuable resource. Time is a commodity that each of us would run out of even if we were miraculously given extra hours each day. Time is a resource that all of us would find a use for and could use a lot more of.

Which of us hasn't caught ourselves feeling "I'm stressed out, burned out, overscheduled and overcommitted". Which of us have never felt the strain and drain of everyone we know wanting and needing our undivided attention all at the exact same time. Who of us doesn't have the mobile ring the very minute we step into the shower?  Without question, time is and will continue to be in limited supply.

The reality is that for each of us and out of our control is the fact that time lost can never be regained. Benjamin Franklin said " Do not squander time; for that's the stuff life is made of."

Do you ever wonder how we got to a place in our history where in today's society we have the most sophisticated technologies known and available to man to help us save time, manage time, control time, make time, keep time, and avoid losing or wasting time?

Yet not withstanding being surrounded by all these high tech, low touch, labor saving devices, we're working harder and longer than ever before in our history. We have less time for our families and for ourselves.

One of the most frustrating things about life today is the fact that there just isn't time to do everything we would like to try or spend time with everyone that we would like to spend time. In fact, in this age of multi tasking, for most of us there is only time to do one or two things on our to do list really well. Everything else on our to do list is a checklist item. It is nothing more than a time consumption activity that pays very little return on our investment.

Here is what the Lord has to say about **Time management** in His word.

(1) In **Matthew 6:33** - but seek first the kingdom of God and his righteousness, and all these things will be added to you.

(2) In **Ephesians 5:15 -17** - Be very careful, then, how you live--not as unwise but as wise, making the most of every

opportunity, because the days are evil. Therefore do not be foolish, but understand what the Lord's will is.

(3) In **Ecclesiastes 3:8** - A time to love, and a time to hate, a time for war, and a time for peace.

(4) Paul considers us wise if we are "redeeming the time, because the days are evil" **(Ephesians 5:16).** He encourages Christians to measure and make use of our time carefully.

So in the end, how exactly do you plan your life so that when it's finished, you don't have regrets for what you failed to accomplish, which was important for you to reach your dreams, aspirations, and goals.

**Here are Eight (8) tips to better manage your time:**

1. **PUT GOD FIRST-** Christ must be at the center of everything. The Bible teaches us that our one and only priority is to keep Him, His Kingdom, and His righteousness first in everything. His will and our service to Him is our priority.

2. **Simplify your life-** Don't allow time demands to burn you out or, worse, feel like a failure because you've pulled up short of your expectations.

3. **Set boundaries-** Be realistic with your time and energy, prioritize what is truly important.

4. **Disconnect-** Take a technology break. Don't think twice about turning off your cell phone and computer

5. **Keep lists-** Lists also keep you organized.

6. **Prioritize and Organized-** Effective time management requires that we get those items with the highest priority accomplished first, affording us to get the greatest ROI

from our available time. Deciding on priorities can be a mind-numbing process. If you want to control your time, then it is time for you to prioritize and to get organized.

7. **Plan-** Develop an action plan to deal with the issue of controlling your time more effectively.

8. **Decide-** Make a decision about what is the best use of your time. To what do you want to devote this precious commodity?

As you consider and decide just what you are going to spend your time on, I would like you to consider that some of your time may be best spent doing nothing and being still. Yes I said it; disciplined stillness is an integral part of time management. Setting aside time to think, plan, listen and speak with the Father is critical if you are to truly control and manage your time. There are times when setting aside quiet time is as important as setting aside time to accomplish some activity.

As you consciously set time aside to listen to the Lord, you may actually hear something? Something that just might make a major difference in the path you choose to put your life on.

Constant daily prayer is in fact encouraged so please don't confuse speaking daily with the Lord with the practice of stillness. The fact remains that for most of us prayer time is our opportunity to speak with the Father. This isn't about any activity including prayer it is about no activity. I am speaking specifically about time where you do nothing except listen. You may be asking yourself listen to what? I am suggesting that you manage this portion of your time to listen for something. Something that you couldn't possible hear above the clutter of your own voice. Something so amazing that it may alter your life and your decision path for all eternity. Is that worth allocating time to?

**Six (6) Questions to better Time Management:**

1.  How well do you believe you control your time now? a) Not well, b) Occasionally well, c) Very well.  Tell me why.

2.  Overall, do you feel that you are in control of how you spend your time, or do you feel that other things or other people are more in control of your time than you are?

3.  Who, or what, then, do you feel is most in control of your time right now?

4.  What would you like to be doing with (some of) your time, that you are not doing now?

5.  If you could change anything about your use of your time, from now on, what would it be?

6.  What is the one thing you could actually do now, to give you more control over your time?

Controlling your time in today's…. got to do it all…now society requires a disciplined approach to life. Decide to give these six (6) steps listed earlier an opportunity to make a difference in your path to a more successful life.

As a final thought on this subject, I would like to suggest that you consciously make a decision to, " not run aimlessly" and put God first. After all, we are commanded to put God first in every area of life (**Matthew 22, Mark 12, Luke 10**). When your life is Christ-centered, time management is put in its proper perspective. At the end of the day, using your time wisely will allow you to place your head on the pillow and sleep contentedly as you will feel good about your day, contribution and life.

**PRACTICE:** To practice this skill keep a daily schedule of what you want to do each day this week…Hour by hour. Write it down. After you have completed your list, make a check mark by each and every activity that was a total waste of your time and energy. Then, develop an action plan to deal with the issue of controlling your time more effectively.

**PRAYER:** Heavenly Father all honor, praise and glory to you. Thank you for the many blessings that you have chosen to provide in my life. Father, your servant, friend, and disciple Paul considers us wise if we are "redeeming the time, because the days are evil" **(Ephesians 5:16).** He encourages Christians to measure and make use of our time carefully. I come to you recognizing that our time on earth is limited, as such, Father I seek your guidance to insure that I respect and utilize the time you provide to your glory and honor. I chose to utilize my time first and foremost to obey your will. Thank you Father for being here for me. I love you Lord.

*To understand the true definition and example of Christian leadership we need look no further than the word, walk, and way of our Lord Jesus. His life of leadership was defined by His eager desire to serve His people and His disciples. In His life, as told to us through the Bible, we find the perfect description of a Christian leader. We are taught that Jesus willingly, knowingly, and lovingly took on the role of leader to all those in his care. Jesus knew well that without His leadership example that we are rudderless.*

# CHAPTER SEVEN

## LEADERSHIP

**"I want to know God's thoughts... the rest are details."**

**Albert Einstein**

Great leaders don't talk a great game, they don't rest on their past accomplishments. They are keenly aware that the size of their office or the title on their business card doesn't entitle them to leadership. They don't take advantage of those who they are entrusted to lead.

Real leaders don't accept credit for successes but recognize that all credit is due to the Father. Real leaders are encouragers and equippers. Real leaders faithfully consider the long term and short-term implications of each and every decision they render and the impact that it will have on the lives of those that surround them.

To understand the true definition and example of Christian leadership, we need look no further than the word, walk, and way of our Lord Jesus. His life of leadership was defined by His eager desire to serve His people and His disciples. In His life, as told to us through the Bible, we find the perfect description of a Christian leader. We are taught that Jesus willingly, knowingly, and lovingly took on the role of leader to all those in his care. Jesus knew well that without His leadership example that we are rudderless.

From His example, we know that a real leader leads, feeds, nurtures, comforts, corrects, directs, and protects.

Leadership by example requires us to model godliness and righteousness in our own life. By example of Salt and Light, real leadership encourages others to follow Jesus.

Christian leaders boldly follow Christ and through both witness and example inspiring others to follow Him as well. The Christian leaders ultimate concern is to follow the Word of God producing strong, faithful Christians.

Here is what the Lord has to say about **Leadership** in His word.

(1) In **TITUS 1:9** - " He must hold firmly to the trustworthy message as it has been taught, so that he can encourage others by sound doctrine and refute those who oppose it."

(2) In **ISAIAH 58:7** - "Is it not to share your food with the hungry and to provide the poor wanderer with shelter—when you see the naked, to clothe him and not to turn away from your own flesh and blood?"

(3) In **DANIEL 2:30** - "As for me, this mystery has been revealed to me, not because I have greater wisdom than other living men, but so that you, O king, may know the interpretation and that you may understand what went through your mind."

(4) In **JOHN 13:5** - "After that, he poured water into a basin and began to wash his disciples' feet, drying them with the towel that was wrapped around him."

(5) In **Matthew 11:27-29** -"All things have been committed to me by my Father. No one knows the Son except the Father, and no one knows the Father except the Son and those to whom the Son chooses to reveal him.

Come to me, all you who are weary and burdened, and I will give you rest. Take my yoke upon you and learn from me, for I am gentle and humble in heart, and you will find rest for your souls."

(6) In **1 TIMOTHY 5:17** - " The elders who direct the affairs of the church well are worthy of double honor, especially those whose work is preaching and teaching."

(7) In **1 PETER 5:3** – "not lording it over those entrusted to you, but being examples to the flock."

(8) In **Matthew 18: 1-4**- " At that time the disciples came to Jesus and asked, "Who is the greatest in the kingdom of heaven?" He called a little child and had him stand among them. And he said: "I tell you the truth, unless you change and become like little children, you will never enter the kingdom of heaven. Therefore, whoever humbles himself like this child is the greatest in the kingdom of heaven."

(9) In **MATTHEW 20:25-28** - "Jesus called them together and said, "You know that the rulers of the Gentiles lord it over them, and their high officials exercise authority over them.

Not so with you. Instead, whoever wants to become great among you must be your servant, and whoever wants to be first must be your slave— just as the Son of Man did not come to be served, but to serve, and to give his life as a ransom for many."

(10) In **1SAMUEL 8:7** - " And the LORD told him: "Listen to all that the people are saying to you; it is not you they have rejected, but they have rejected me as their king."

(11) In **2 TIMOTHY 3:16-17** –" All Scripture is God-breathed and is useful for teaching, rebuking, correcting and training in righteousness, so that the man of God may be thoroughly equipped for every good work."

(12) In **JOHN 10:11**- "I am the good shepherd. The good shepherd lays down his life for the sheep."

Through out the ages, history is replete with stories of amazing leaders who made an incredible impact on the lives of people in their own time and on our lives today.

History also documents that as important as these men were, there was always a new one to pick up where the last one left off. Except for one, that one was the leader of leaders. That one was Jesus Christ.

The biblical term for leader is Lord. As our leader, we should be looking for direction in our lives from the Father. Not being one to ever disappoint His children, His way, walk, word, and life provide us with a lifetime of examples to draw from.

If you want to learn how to lead, you must first serve a great leader. That leader who will guide and direct you in all phases of leadership training is Jesus Christ. As you lead, always look to the Father for guidance. By investing your time and effort in His word, you will always have a rock to stabilize you and a blue print for successful leadership.

As our leader, the Savior does not follow our lead. He doesn't wait for our approval of His plan. As the leader, He makes it clear that we are called to follow Him and His lead. He for certain provides us with leadership opportunities by all such opportunities are guided by His wisdom, plan and leadership.

To this end, we do not invite and then lead God to join in our plan. No, if we are chosen, He honors us with an invitation to join Him in His activity on His terms. We are guided by His will not ours.

So in the end, real leadership runs deep in those who surrender, serve, and seek the will of God. Real leaders live the word of God to all whom cross their path.

Their lives are the definition of Salt and Light. Real leaders possess His spirit in their words, actions, decisions, deeds, and hearts.

In those instances, where leaders encounter a conflict between the word, will, or way of God and the path being traveled they immediately seek His will and put in place a corrective action plan. Without hesitation, they stand up to be counted.

Real leaders are not concerned with being politically correct. Real leaders never leave people on the wrong path going in the wrong direction.

**Here are Seven (7) tips to Real Leadership:**

1. **PUT GOD FIRST-** Christ must be at the center of everything. The Bible teaches us that our one and only priority is to keep Him, His Kingdom, and His righteousness first in everything. His will and our service to Him is our priority.

2. **Focus-** Be specific about the decisions, direction and objectives, which you establish.

3. **Create a Vision**- Make decisions that communicate your dreams, your passions, and your intended actions.

4. **Take Responsibility and Set Direction** - You control your decision to lead, follow, or get out of the way. If you truly believe in your abilities, it is your responsibility to work with others to set direction.

5. **Establish Goals, Objectives, and Plans**- Words, and speeches don't make the man or the leader. Action and results do. Get to work.

6 **Care Enough to Influence Direction** – To lead effectively, you have to care about those you are attempting to lead. It is not about you. It is about them. If the troops don't know that you care, you will not be their leader.

7. **Listen to Learn**- Leaders listen and talkers talk. Listen; Think, Listen, Think, Talk.

It seems that these days leadership is a very popular, hot topic as there are countless seminars, articles, and self help books written on the subject. Becoming a successful leader is the topic of much discussion. According to popular teaching, successful leaders must be blessed with the skills and talents to communicate a vision and set goals for people or an organization to follow.

That being the case, the most famous and successful leaders of our age all recognized that human wisdom can never match God's leadership and direction. These leaders recognized the leadership, guidance, and hand of the Lord in these matters. Christian leaders realize and acknowledge that they are the conduits but that God is the leader of our lives and our family.

## Six (6) Questions to Real Leadership:

1.  Would you say that others typically consider you a leader? What makes you think that?

2.  When you think of the term "Leadership" what thoughts come to your mind – overall, what are your attitudes about real "Leadership"?

3.  What is the last act of Leadership you demonstrated?

4.  In what area of your life do you demonstrate the most leadership?

5.  In what area of your life do you demonstrate the least leadership?

6.  If you wanted to improve your leadership skills, what is one thing you could do, starting now, to achieve that?

I want to encourage you to take a step back and take a long, hard, look at your life. Are you being called to leadership? If so, it is the leader's responsibility to obey the Father as he leads those in his path to Christ likeness.

The Father knows what is best and He takes responsibility for all. As leaders, our responsibility is to faithfully perform the role that He has chosen and assigned to us.

To successfully lead others through the chaos of confusion, that is constantly thrust upon us daily, we need to find a rock that stabilizes and secures us. I would suggest that you would find that rock in Jesus.

Consider these Ten (10) Qualities and Skills to put you on the path to Real Leadership.

## Ten (10) Leadership Qualities and Skills:

| **Leadership qualities** | **Leadership Skills** |
|---|---|
| 1) Accountability | 6) Motivation |
| 2) Decision making | 7) Delegation |
| 3) Communication | 8) Manage |
| 4) Integrity | 9) Organize |
| 5) Confidence | 10) Plan |

As a final thought on this subject, those whom God calls as leaders are expected to exhibit great humility and be willing servants who have aligned their will with that of the Father. Those who are chosen to lead God's people must above all be blessed with the gifts of sacrifice, devotion, submission, and lowliness.

Jesus Himself gave us the pattern when He took on the responsibility of the lowest of lowly slaves that being the foot washer and washed the feet of His disciples.

If the Lord, who designed and created the universe and every cell on it, would chose to take on the role and responsibility of servant hood, clearly those chosen to leadership should follow His example.

Commit today to learn how to become the Real Leader you were destined to be.

**PRACTICE:** To practice the concept of leadership this week, I'd like you to make a list in your Success Journal of three areas that others most always look to you to lead. Then take some time to consider how you work, act, talk differently about these subjects, write an action step telling yourself how you could accomplish that level of leadership in other areas of your life.

**PRAYER:** Heavenly Father all honor, praise and glory to you. Thank you for the many blessings that you have chosen to provide. Father your years on this earth were a tutorial about leadership. Every act, each decision, all-teaching and commands were all to lead us by example. Thank you Lord for loving us so much that you willingly, knowingly, and lovingly shed your blood for us. Thank you Father for being my rock. I love you Lord.

*Regarding the emotion of fear. Our heavenly Father minces no words. He teaches us that the only fear that God encourages in a Christian's life is the fear of God. A healthy fear of the Father is encouraged to demonstate the love, respect, gratefulness, thankfulness, honor and esteem that we hold Him. After all, he only created everything we see, hear, smell, touch, know and have yet to learn.*

# CHAPTER EIGHT

## DEALING WITH FEAR

**"You can conquer almost any fear if you will only make up your mind to do so. For remember, fear doesn't exist anywhere except in the mind."**

**Dale Carnegie**

Regarding the emotion of fear, our heavenly Father minces no words. He teaches us that the only fear that God encourages in a Christian's life is the fear of God. A healthy fear of the Father is encouraged to demonstrate the love, respect, gratefulness, thankfulness, honor and esteem that we hold Him. After all he only created everything we see, hear, smell, touch, know and have yet to learn.

So let's get right at it. Of what are you fearful? Is it losing your job, losing your figure, losing the respect of your family, losing a competitive sporting event? Is it fear of being loved, the fear of rejection, the fear of giving your whole heart to another?

Is it the fear of commitment, the fear of failure, the fear of success, or the fear of rejection? Are your fears affecting and/or effecting your Christ-centered life and decision process? Search your heart and enter your own fear(s) here.

If your answer is that you fear nothing, I know that is the expected macho answer, it is not personal but I will have to call you on the truth of that answer. The reality is that at one time or another, we all have or do fear something.

In fact, most of us deal regularly with the fact that we fear many things that we need not and should not fear. Fear is a cancer to our successes, often keeping us from successfully pursuing our goals, aspirations, and dreams.

The good news is that the list of things that we should fear is extremely short. So short in fact that only God is on it. The Bible is clear that out of respect we should fear God. Each of us should fear that the conduct of our lives would be disappointing to our heavenly Father. We should fear not living up to the standard our Father has set for us. We should fear making decisions that restrict us from reaching the plan, purpose and potential that He has planned for us

The bottom line and the liberating news is that we need only fear one thing and one thing only. That one legitimate fear we should have is in fact a healthy fear of God.

So aside from God, what illegitimate fear do you harbor?

The truth about fear is that it zaps our energy, reduces confidence, and enslaves us. Fear is weakness that drains our strength. Fear both creates the environment of and is failure. Fear arises as a direct result of our insecurities. Fear results from our desire to feed our ego. It results from our insecurity and need to have others think that we are winners. Fear is the direct result of not trusting the word, commitment, and oath of our Father. Fear freezes our ability to make decisions when they need to be made. Fear causes us to lose valuable opportunities. Fear reduces our opportunity for success. Fear stinks!

It is important to think about, remember, and hold on to with a death grip that the fear of situations, outcomes and people does not come from God. We must each come to terms with the reality that fear heightens our imaginations and can magnify a depth and width of a problem until it seems insurmountable.

Fortunately for us, the good news is that there is no reason to live in fear when you have a personal relationship with God. If you have decided to trust the Father, then fear not.

**Here is what the Lord has to say about Dealing With Fear in His word.**

(1) In **Genesis 15:1** - "Do not be afraid, Abram. I am your shield, your very great reward."

(2) In **Joshua 1:9** - "Have I not commanded you? Be strong and courageous. Do not be terrified; do not be discouraged, for the LORD your God will be with you wherever you go."

(3) In **Judges 7:3** - announce now to the people, 'Anyone who trembles with fear may turn back and leave Mount Gilead.' " So twenty-two thousand men left, while ten thousand remained.

(4) In **Psalm 23:4** - "Even though I walk through the valley of the shadow of death, I will fear no evil, for you are with me; your rod and your staff, they comfort me."

(5) In **Isaiah 41:10** - "So do not fear, for I am with you; do not be dismayed, for I am your God. I will strengthen you and help you; I will uphold you with my righteous right hand."

(6) In **2 Timothy 1:7** - "For God has not given us a spirit of fear, but of power and of love and of a sound mind."

(7) In **1 John 4:18** - "There is no fear in love. But perfect love drives out fear, because fear has to do with punishment. The one who fears is not made perfect in love."

(8) In **Hebrews 13** - "So we say with confidence, "The Lord is my helper; I will not be afraid. What can man do to me?"

(9) In **2 Corinthians 5:10-11** - "For we must all appear before the judgment seat of Christ, that each one may receive what is due him for the things done while in the body, whether good or bad. Since, then, we know what it is to fear the Lord, we try to persuade men. What we are is plain to God, and I hope it is also plain to your conscience."

(10) In **John 14:26-27** - "But the Counselor, the Holy Spirit, whom the Father will send in my name, will teach you all things and will remind you of everything I have said to you. Peace I leave with you; my peace I give you. I do not give to you as the world gives. Do not let your hearts be troubled and do not be afraid."

**Here are Six (6) tips to Deal with Fear:**

1. **PUT GOD FIRST-** Christ must be at the center of everything. The Bible teaches us that our one and only priority is to keep Him, His Kingdom, and His righteousness first in everything. His will and our service to Him is our priority.

2. **Identify and Address your Core Fear-** What are you fearful of and why do you fear it?

3. **Change your Thought Process-** Get Positive in thought and word. Negativity breeds fear. You will never get passed your fear until you believe that you have nothing to fear except fear itself.

4. **Study positive, affirming scripture** – Memorize and recite the scripture referenced above. It will give you the confidence and strength to deal with your fear. Pray persistently.

5. **Use Biblical Solutions to deal with the Fear-** What does the Bible say about how to deal with the Fear? Follow His word and way and everything will turn out for the good.

6. **Faithfully Pray** - Seek a constant personal relationship with your heavenly Father. Take the time to actually ask your Father to guide your decision process. With committed, trusting friends, associates, accountability partners and family at our sides, learn how to truly seek His will. God will free us from the past, handle the day-to-day pressures in the present and move forward to the future He has planned.

Fear and worry go hand in hand. Both affect our willingness and confidence to take chances on ourselves. Although both fear and worry are unavoidable, we do possess the ability and strength to limit the amount of damage that we allow them to extract and the number of opportunities lost as a result of their negative influence in our lives. Make a decision today to deal with your fears head up. Refuse to back down.

**Six Questions To Deal With Fear:**

1. Would you rate yourself as: a) Seldom afraid, b) Occasionally afraid, or c) Often afraid? Why?

2. How do you typically react to something you fear? (Examples – avoid, confront, ignore, freeze up etc.)

3. In what ways do you feel fear works for you?

4. In what ways do you feel fear works against you?

5. What is one thing you could do, more often, to overcome fears that keep you from doing something you should do, or from dealing with something you should deal with?

6. If you wrote one goal about fear, what would you say?

To effectively deal with fear, we need to have both a strong sense of self-confidence and a clear mind in order that we might see and understand events in their proper perspective. The problem that all too often arises is that many individuals fear what people think and say about them far more than they fear disappointing God.

The result of this thought process ends being that our fears, the need to appease others who cross our path, and our internal conflict over how others view us end up being a hindrance from our ability to take the steps necessary to please God. The clutter of all this confusion makes it all but impossible to make decisions that we feel good about.

So in the end it is clear that fear results from our personal insecurities of both the known and unknown. We know that fear gets in the way and causes us to stop, second guess, and question the sovereignty of God's will.

In His word, Jesus instructs us that fear results from straying from God's word and way. The good news is that based upon the Bible, His word frees us from all fear and admonishes us that the only fear that God encourages in a Christian's life is the fear of God.

With that being said, fear, the negative and often debilitating emotional responses that often accompany it, should not be allowed to interfere with our decision-making or the success that springs from sound decisions.

As a final thought on this subject, there is no reason to live in fear when you have a personal relationship with the Father.

Pray to God that He frees you from any fear that you are experiencing and to open your eyes to the truth. As He reveals the reality of the situation, He will enable you to over come your fear.

**PRACTICE:** To practice these skills consider making a list of three unnecessary, irrational fears that you experience most. Once this is accomplished, develop a short action step for dealing with each of these. This skill is very important to develop as often fear of the unknown, or what we can't control often are the elements that prevent us from getting those real answers, real solutions, and real results which we desire and expect when we make decisions.

**PRAYER:** Heavenly Father, all honor, praise and glory to you. Your name is a mighty tower of strength and all who run to it are both safe and saved. Thank you for the many blessings that you have chosen to provide in my life. Father In **Isaiah 41:10** you mix no words **"So do not fear, for I am with you; do not be dismayed, for I am your God. I will strengthen you and help you; I will uphold you with my righteous right hand."** I come to you seeking only your love and the strength that comes from that love. With you watching over me I fear not, forging forward doing your work. Thank you Father for being here for me. In Jesus' name.

*Prioritizing skills demonstrates your ability to see what tasks, or areas of your life are worthy of your attention, energy, resources and time. Prioritizing is about making decisions on choices of what to do and what not to do. To prioritize effectively, you need to be able to recognize what is important, as well as to see the difference between urgent, important, and a nuisance.*

# Chapter Nine

## PRIORITIZING EFFECTIVELY

**"You need a plan to build a house. To build a life, it is even more important to have a plan or goal."**

**Zig Ziglar**

Prioritizing effectively is at its core based upon the ability to make solid, long-term decisions. Prioritizing effectively cannot exist without time management and time management cannot exist without it. Prioritizing effectively should be viewed as our skill to manage and control ourselves in relationship to date, time and event. It is setting priorities and taking charge of our long-term and short-term goals. It is being skilled in the area of aligning our long and short-term goals.

Prioritizing effectively requires us to make the necessary corrections to reduce if not eliminate those habits, practices, and activities that cause us to waste energy, time, and opportunity. It is the willingness and flexibility to experiment with different concepts and ideas enabling us to make maximum use of our time and decision making ability.

The often-sighted Pareto Rule states that 80 percent of our routine activities contribute less than 20 percent to the outcome of our desired results. Given the truth in this statement, it is imperative that each of us prioritizes our decisions, projects, and tasks in order to achieve more efficiency.

Focusing on top priority decisions is the easiest way to improve personal productivity, attain long-term goals, and reach ultimate success.

The skill to prioritize effectively begins with the ability to make long-term decisions on what you desire most in life and then effectively and efficiently organizing your time and activities to achieve that goal. For maximum effectiveness to result, every action decided upon must involve the most efficient use of our time and effort in achieving those objectives.

If you are at all like me, you know how easy it is to fall into the trap of spending a day attending unexpected interruptions, phone calls, and e-mails. As a result of the time pollution, we miss out on the opportunity to use our day to complete more important tasks, which pay a higher long-term investment and provide us with greater satisfaction.

Prioritizing effectively saves time, resources and energy. Mastering our prioritizing skills increases our ability to examine and determine which tasks are critical for long-term success while affording us the luxury of allowing our attention, energy, resources and time to be spent more effectively. Prioritizing allows us to utilize all these efforts, skills, and talents on successfully attaining all of our long-term goals. This process when done well places focus and attention on what is important at the expense of less important activities.

Prioritizing is about making choices of what to do, what not to do, and when to do it. Prioritizing effectively requires the ability to recognize what is important long-term and short-term, as well as the ability to identify the difference between critical, urgent, important, nice, and unnecessary.

Here is what the Lord has to say about **Prioritizing** in His word.

(1) In **Luke 10:41-42** - "Martha, Martha," the Lord answered, "you are worried and upset about many things, but only one thing is needed. Mary has chosen what is better, and it will not be taken away from her."

(2) In **Matthew 6:31-33** -"So do not worry, saying, 'What shall we eat?' or 'What shall we drink?' or 'What shall we wear? 'For the pagans run after all these things, and your heavenly Father knows that you need them.

But seek first his kingdom and his righteousness, and all these things will be given to you as well."

(3) In **Matthew 6:19** - "Do not store up for yourselves treasures on earth, where moth and rust destroy, and where thieves break in and steal."

(4) In **Luke 12:15** - "Then he said to them, "Watch out! Be on your guard against all kinds of greed; a man's life does not consist in the abundance of his possessions."

(5) In **Matthew 5:6** - "Blessed are those who hunger and thirst for righteousness, for they will be filled."

(6) In **Psalms 1:1-2** - "Blessed is the man who does not walk in the counsel of the wicked or stand in the way of sinners or sit in the seat of mockers. But his delight is in the law of the LORD, and on his law he meditates day and night."

(7) In **Revelation 4:11** - "You are worthy, our Lord and God to receive glory and honor and power, for you created all things, and by your will they were created and have their being."

(8) In **Colossians 1:16** - "For by him all things were created: things in heaven and on earth, visible and invisible, whether thrones or powers or rulers or authorities; all things were created by him and for him.

(9) In **Ephesians 4:22-24** - "You were taught, with regard to your former way of life, to put off your old self, which is being corrupted by its deceitful desires; to be made new in the attitude of your minds; and to put on the new self, created to be like God in true righteousness and holiness."

(10) In **Colossians 3:9-10** - "Do not lie to each other, since you have taken off your old self with its practices and have put on the new self, which is being renewed in knowledge in the image of its Creator."

(11) In **John 1:1** - "In the beginning was the Word, and the Word was with God, and the Word was God."

(12) In **Titus 2:11-12**- "or the grace of God that bring salvation hath appeared to all men, Teaching us that, denying ungodliness and worldly lusts, we should live soberly, righteously, and godly, in this present world"

So in the end, mastering the skill of prioritizing effectively is a difficult challenge but one that will make a positive difference in your decision making ability. Without the ability to prioritize tasks and schedules, most of us will find ourselves feeling overwhelmed, stressed, unhappy, and lacking focus throughout the day. By prioritizing your life, you can focus on what is really important and finish the day with a true sense of accomplishment, direction, and victory.

**Here are Seven (7) tips to Prioritizing Effectively:**

1. **PUT GOD FIRST-** Christ must be at the center of everything. The Bible teaches us that our one and only priority is to keep Him, His Kingdom, and His righteousness first in everything. His will and our service to Him is our priority.

2. **Focus-** Be specific about the decisions, goals and objectives which you establish so that you are moving in the direction of something of value and passion to you. Remember that many people commit 110% to climb the ladder of success, only to find that it is leaning against the wrong building.

3. **Take a Long Term View-** Make decisions in the present that can have the greatest positive impact on your future. Short- term decisions must align themselves with established long-term decisions.

4. **Measure Twice and Cut Once -** Be sure to take the time to do your work right the first time. The fewer mistakes you make, the less time you will waste going back and correcting it.

5. **Keep Lists-** What counts is not the quantity of time that you put into a project or decision but rather the amount of time that you spend working on high-priority project or decision. Lists keep you organized.

6 **Prioritize and Organized -** Understand that the most important factor in setting priorities is your ability to make solid decisions. Prioritizing effectively requires that we get those items with the highest priority accomplished first, affording us to get the greatest ROI from our available time.

7. **Plan-** Set clear priorities for each area of your life. Remember to always make the decision to choose the

activities that will assure you the greatest health, happiness and financial success in the long term. Develop an action plan to help you more effectively set priorities.

## Six (6) Questions to better Effective Priority Setting:

1. How would you rate yourself right now, with regard to setting priorities overall? a) Very good, b) Average, c) Needs work.   (Why did you give yourself that rating?)

2. How much time, on an average day, do you take to set specific priorities for that day?   (Why?)

3. Who, or what, do you feel is most responsible for determining your priorities?   (Why?)

4. Do you feel, in general, that you spend the majority of your time doing what you would choose to do, if not, what are you spending your time on?   (Why?)

5. Do you believe that you have a clear picture of what your real priorities are?   (Write down why you know that and what they are.)

6. Do you feel there is anything you would like to do, to manage your priorities in a better way?

Each of us has experienced urgent, unexpected and critical events that threaten to overwhelm established and set priorities for our day and lives. Each and everyday with are confronted with decisions which threaten to redirect our energies and priorities. In reaction to these curveballs, we often over react by setting plans and priorities in stone that end up being too rigid and inflexible to respond quickly to changes in daily conditions. We usually over react moving towards inflexibility when we don't take or make the time to constantly reevaluate the success of our priorities. On the other hand forging forward with no plans at all is risky, ineffective, and unprofessional.

More often than not total flexibility serves only to produce total chaos in our day and in our lives.

To successfully deal with the chaos of confusion that is constantly thrust upon us daily, each of us should be equipped and trained to create a workable process for prioritizing effectively that has a long term vision, is flexible enough to adapt to inevitable daily challenges, and is stable enough to provide security and direction.

Prioritizing effectively in our, **I need it done now,** society requires a disciplined approach to each decision, each project, each relationship, each and every day of our life?

Consider these Five (5) Pitfalls to avoid to make a difference in your path to both make more effective decisions and to live a more successful life.

**Five (5) Priority Setting Pitfalls to avoid:**

1) **First Come First Serve** - Do not allow yourself to get caught up in the e-mail mentality of setting your priorities simply by responding to things as they happen? If you set your priorities first come, first serve, you are not choosing your priorities; your priorities are really choosing you.

2) **Self- Delegation** - Don't be fearful to invest the time or money necessary to train someone who can take on some of the lower-priority tasks that you are currently performing?

3) **Whose are Hot** – Make certain that you are clear with everyone that regardless of the heat of the discussion/ request his or her priorities will not become your priority. In all cases, your priorities will remain your priorities.

4) **This Won't Take Long** – Always tackle high priority decisions and tasks first. Avoid convincing yourself that

you can clear out all the other mess first, as it won't take that long, and then you can concentrate on the important things.

**5 When I Feel Like it** – High priority decisions and goals won't always be the easiest or most pleasant tasks on your list, but dig in and tackle them first.

As a final thought on this subject, I would like you to consider that prioritizing effectively saves you time, resources and energy.

In addition, as prioritizing is a decision on to itself, it puts you on the road to great decision-making. Prioritizing skills demonstrates your ability to see what tasks, or areas of your life are worthy of your attention, energy, resources and time. Prioritizing is about making decisions on choices of what to do and what not to do.

To prioritize effectively, you need to be able to recognize what is important, as well as to see the difference between urgent, important, and a nuisance.

**PRACTICE:** To practice the concept of prioritizing this week, I'd like you to list any and all priorities that raise their head. In your Success Journal, make a list of everything you see as a priority in your life right now – short term and long term. Take some time with this – it's worth it. You can't know what you really want or don't want, until you write the list.

**PRAYER:** Heavenly Father all honor, praise and glory to you. Your name is a mighty tower of strength and all who run to it are both safe and saved. Thank you for the many blessings that you have chosen to provide in my life. Father In **John 1:1** it is confirmed that **"In the beginning was the Word, and the Word was with God, and the Word was God."** I come to you we the knowledge that you were first and as such all my priorities begin with placing you first, foremost, and top of mind. Once I have appropriately sought and prioritized your will all other matters fall in to place successfully. Thank you Father for being here for me. I love you Lord.

*Bottom line is that being successful starts with uncovering your God given skills and talents and then moving on to discover how you can best use your strengths, gifts, talents and abilities to fulfill His purpose for your life.*

# Chapter Ten

## UTILIZING YOUR SKILLS AND TALENTS

**"When I stand before God at the end of my life, I would hope that I would not have a single bit of talent left, and could say, "I used everything you gave me."**

**Erma Louise Bombeck**

Do you recall George Brett, Hall of fame, Kansas City Royal, pine tar incident and one of baseballs all time great hitters and players?

Without question, George knew how to utilize his skills and talents to the maximum. I read a story a while back about George that really placed the concept of using our skills and talents to their maximum into its proper focus and light.

The story goes that post retirement George Brett was being interviewed. Not an uncommon event either then or today for George. George was asked an uncommon question albeit one that ended up speaking directly to his greatness.

The question that he was asked was if he could write the script for the last at bat of his career, what would he have penned?

After thinking about it for not more than a second or two George replied, I would want to hit a scorching routine ground ball to an infielder, second or short, I run full speed down the base path only to be thrown out at first by less than a step.

The interviewer who was caught completely off guard by this answer responded with a puzzled… really. You mean he went on, you wouldn't have wanted to end your career with a game winning hit or better yet maybe a walk off game winning home run? George replied that no, it would definitely be a scorching routine ground ball, I would run my hardest, giving it all that I had only to be thrown out with a close bang, bang play at first base.

The interviewer at this point completely perplexed and not really knowing what to make of George's answer could only think to ask, why?

George responded this way; well, a home run is always great and it is true that a home run to win a game on my last at bat is the stuff, which the movies are made. But I hit a lot of home runs in my career and I have been fortunate to have a career blessed with clutch hits.

I guess I kind of feel that most all baseball fans know that I can hit the ball pretty good.

If I hit a home run, I am going to jog victoriously around the bases and that would be a cool moment and all but, if I hit a routine scorcher to an infielder all these fans, especially the younger fans, are going to witness that on the last at bat of my career, with absolutely nothing left to prove, that I still loved the battle and the game enough that I utilized my skills and talents to the maximum, to the end.

On my last at bat of my career, I am more interested that everyone in the ballpark and on ESPN see me hustling down the base path at full speed than I am to have them see me jogging around them half speed.

That is how I want to end my career and my legacy remembered.

As we discuss utilizing your skills and talents, remember the words of George Brett. We have a responsibility to use our God given skills and talents to the maximum having left nothing on the table.

That is our calling, our purpose and our responsibility.

Have you ever slowed down long enough to objectively evaluate your personal strengths, gifts, skills, talents and abilities? Have you thought about how often you actually put them to use? Do you find yourself spending a majority of your brainpower identifying your weaknesses and investing most of your energies trying to figure out just how to overcome these imperfections? If your answer to this question is affirmative, I need to alert you to the fact that this tendency is very detrimental to your spirit and totally takes away from your strengths and talents. A little compulsion towards perfection can be healthy but you don't need to venture far down that path to get to the town of negativity and destruction.

Each of us is blessed to have a unique set of skills and talents given to us by the Father. These skills were given to us to fulfill His long-term plan for our lives. When we discover the value and promise of our talents and learn how to capitalize on them, we position ourselves to achieve a lot of success in life. Successes that the Father expects each of us to relentlessly seek and attain. His promise for our lives is iron clad, all we have to do is surrender to His will and allow Him to use us for His purpose and plan.

Some skills seem to come naturally to us, while others have formulated and developed as a direct result of the activities, jobs, experiences and interests we have pursued during the course of our lifetime.

Bottom line is that being successful starts with uncovering your God given skills and talents and then moving on to discover how you can best use your strengths, gifts, talents and abilities to fulfill His purpose for our life.

**Here is what the Lord has to say about Utilizing your Skills and Talents in His word.**

(1) In **Proverbs 18:16** - "A man's gift makes room for him, and brings him before great men."

(2) In **Timothy 4:14** - "Do not neglect the gift that is in you, which was given to you by prophecy with the laying on of the hands of the eldership."

(3) In **Romans 11:29** - "For God's gifts and His call are irrevocable."

(4) In **2 Timothy 1:6** - "Therefore I remind you to stir up the gift of God which is in you through the laying on of my hands."

I assume that you have begun a process of skills assessment with an end goal of deciding what is the most effective use of your skills and talents. If this is the case, begin by relishing in the truth that God has blessed each of us with skills and talents, which are to be used expressly to fulfill His plan and purpose for our life. Not only has He blessed each of us with natural abilities but he has also equipped us with spiritual gifts for the purpose of serving His ministry.

The counter balance to all this great news is the reality that anything, which comes as a blessing, carries with it an obligation. In this case, we are expected to use Gods gifts to benefit His work, His ministry, the lives of our family, loved ones, and all those who He puts on our path.

At this point, if you haven't begun an assessment process ask and answer this question: What skills and talents has God blessed and gifted you with and how is He calling you to use them?

**Here are Six (6) tips to maximize the utilization of your Skills and Talents:**

1. **Each of us is given according to his ability -** God doesn't give us gifts we can't use, or gifts that we can't handle. Use your talents.

2. **Identify Your Unique Skills and Talents-** Recognize, acknowledge, explore and identify strengths and talents.

3. **Each of us is expected to take a risk with our talents** - Be aware that there is no such thing as a "safe" investment when it comes to using our skills. Be realistic as using your talents require a measure of risk be taken in order to get return. Don't be fearful to take a chance. Trust your skill set.

4. **Cultivate your talent -** According to a recent theory, you possess about seven hundred natural skills or talents at birth. But in any given job, you use around seventy skills. Essentially, this means that you draw on about ten percent of your skills at work. Make and take time to develop your skills and talents.

5. **Your talent opens doors of opportunity -** Don't sit around waiting to find a way for you to use your gift. Each of us has at a minimum one gift. Most have several that complement each other. Our gifts are given for the common good, to build up the Body of Christ. As such, your gifts, if used in

accordance with His will, open doors of opportunity and success.

6. **Use Your Skill and Talents Productively** - God knows who will be productive with His gifts, skills and talents. As you prove yourself faithful with what God has given you, He will entrust you with more highly developed skills and opportunities to use them. However, if you don't use the gifts God has blessed you with, He will give them to someone else who will use them productively.

**Six (6) Questions To Productively Using Your Skills and Talents:**

1. Name three of your talents that you have that are most important to you. (And why?)

2. Overall, do you see yourself as: a) Very talented, b) Average when it comes to talents, or c) Having few talents? Why?

3. Do you believe that most talents are "natural" (you're born with them), or do you believe that you create them?

4. Describe a person who is "highly talented." What is that person like?

5. What talents would you most like to possess that you feel you do not have now? What steps are you taking to develop these skills?

6. What talents do you have now, that you would like to work on and develop further?

So in the end, everyone has special gifts and talents that could be utilized to make the world a better place in which to live. In the event that your skill(s) were previously on hold, hidden, or dormant, now is the time to take advantage and enthusiastically pursue them. Using your skills to fulfill His purpose will certainly cause God joy.

On a personal note, making the decision to invest in and use the skills that you have been blessed with will put you in position to attain great results, inner peace and have great fun reaching for that success.

As a final thought on this subject, if you want to make a living out of your skills or talents, you need to provide and market a value that people need and/or desire. So if that is your goal, ask yourself this question. How can you turn your talent into a value that people will pay for? Once you have figured that out, choose to trust your skills and decide how and when to go for the gold.

**PRACTICE:** To practice the concept of talents this week, I'd like you to make a list, in your Success Journal, of every talent you have. Number them in order of importance to you. Then put a check mark by the talents you would like to work on or improve. Also, make a second list of new talents you'd like to have, and rate them in order of their importance to you.

**PRAYER:** Heavenly Father all honor, praise and glory to you. Thank you for the many blessings that you have chosen to provide in my life. Father, you have blessed me with skills and talents and instructed me to use them for Kingdom building. Although my spirit is willing, unfortunately my heart is sometimes weak. I come to you asking that you give me the desire and heart to allow me to use the talents and skills that you have blessed me with to honor your name. Thank you Father for being my rock. I love you Lord.

*I am asking you to consider, as the first step to finding balance, to seek out the will of the Father and commit yourself to living the life that God has planned for you.*

*In order to free yourself up to get to this point in life, a second step that you must take, is to be ready to commit to being disciplined, to surrender to His will, and to devote every aspect of your life; Spiritual, mental, emotional, and physical to finding balance with His will.*

*Attaining this level of surrender and peace requires the complete elimination of any and all excuses in our life. It requires a resolve on our part to be all that the Father has called us to be. It requires that we get focused with a singleness of purpose to align our will with His.*

# CHAPTER ELEVEN

## FINDING LIFE'S BALANCE

**"Most people struggle with life balance simply because they haven't paid the price to decide what is really important to them."**

**Stephen Covey**

Have you ever noticed that engraved on our monetary supply are the words In God We Trust and E pluribus Unum?

Each of us more than likely understands the significant meaning behind our country honoring the financial treasure of the Father but what about E pluribus Unum?

E pluribus Unum is Latin for one out of many. Interesting stuff.

Forgetting what modern day politicians and historians may want to rewrite about our country's history, the fact is that our great leaders knew the significant example of honoring the Father and reminding all that we are taught to follow His example and serve our neighbor with love and humility.

Our great leaders recognized and wanted each of us to be continually reminded that independently we each represent just one and our great strength comes from the many.

This is a country that's tradition is founded on a Judo Christian belief system. Our founding fathers knew how important it was to honor the Father on our monetary supply.

Is it possible that they chose to honor the Father on our country's money because they heeded the Fathers warning of the great distraction, sin, and false God that money can become in our lives?

Is there a message about surrender, service and balance here?

One of the most important ongoing series of decisions that you will have opportunity to wrestle with over the course of your lifetime has to do with whether or not your life is in balance. Do your decisions control your life or are life's events controlling you? This seems like an easy question to answer but I caution you, slow down and think this through as it is a very important question to answer correctly as it will spark a series of important decisions.

I have heard it quoted that: "Leading a balanced life can be difficult for any of us. There is not an exact pattern that works for everyone, and even our own blueprint may change during different phases of life." I think this is a fairly insightful assessment but it seems to me that the real question is what does finding balance mean to you, your decision process, and reaching a true balance in your life?

Let's take just a second slowing down long enough to evaluate the actual balance in your life. Do you find yourself involved in activities that you wouldn't choose to be involved in if you were driving the decision process? Do you find yourself missing key moments in the lives of your family members? Do you feel like you have to be on 24/7/365? Do you feel that nothing happens without you bearing its burden? Does your life feel out of control and heading in a direction not of your choosing? Do you find that your job is a source of concern, frustration, or stress? Do you find yourself under achieving? Do you find yourself not making the decisions that you know that you should be making? Do you find yourself unable to disconnect from your mobile phone, blackberry, and personal computer?

At this point if you are thinking, hey this guy must know me because these questions certainly apply to me. No, we have not met but there is an old adage that misery loves company. So join the crowd brother, like many of us your life can probably use a bit of balance.

This is not a question of right vs. wrong lifestyle but rather a question of effective vs. ineffective lifestyle.

Finding balance in your life is centered on the ability and willingness to prioritize well thought out short and long-term decisions. Balance cannot exist without us choosing to master the skill of managing and controlling ourselves in relationship to date and time. At its core, it requires us to make decisions that we believe in and not allow ourselves to have decisions thrust upon us as a result of the chaos that surrounds our life.

In essence, balance is all about the commitment to keep all people, events, projects, schedules, and activities in appropriate perspective. This requires us to take a firm, bold stand against all the people, habits, practices, and activities that cause us to waste energy, time, resources and opportunity. We have to be courageous, bold and willing to look an opportunity in the eye and say "no thank you", tonight is my night out with my wife, daughter, son, or family.

It is an old business adage that 80 percent of our routine activities contribute less than 20 percent to the outcome of our desired results. The result of the 80-20 rule is that each of us must assume full responsibility and control of our decisions, projects, and tasks in order to find the happy center and balance in our lives. It is the unproductive 80% that eats up our time and robs us of balance in life.

These time consumers rob us of time we cherish with our family and friends, while contributing nearly nothing to our effectiveness or success. Guard with all your might against falling into their trap and allowing these unproductive time consumers to control your time, peace, success, and balance.

Instead, consider reallocating some of the time that you were allotting to this 80 percent crowd to focus on a higher calling, one in which honors the Father, your family, and you. Investing in service of some type, as a priority generally improves balance, frees us up to experience increased personal productivity, attainment of long-term goals, and allows us to reach ultimate success, happiness, and peace of mind.

For all these reasons, I am asking you to consider as the first step to finding balance, to seek out the will of the Father and commit yourself to living the life that God has planned for you.

In order to free yourself up to get to this point in life, a second step that you must take is to be ready to commit to being disciplined, to surrender to His will, and to devote every aspect of your life; Spiritual, mental, emotional, and physical to finding balance with His will.

Attaining this level of surrender and peace requires the complete elimination of any and all excuses in our life. It requires a resolve on our part to be all that the Father has called us to be. It requires that we get focused with a singleness of purpose to align our will with His.

With this accomplished, we can position our life to take advantage of His promises.

Pray for guidance as you seek to put Him first and prioritize your life so that you can find the inner peace, security and love of balance.

Here is what the Lord has to say about **Finding Balance In Life** in His word.

(1) In **Job 31:6** - "Let me be weighed in an even balance, that God may know mine integrity."

(2) In **Proverbs 11:1** - "A false balance is abomination to the Lord: but a just weight is his delight."

(3) In **Matthew 6:33** - " But seek first his kingdom and his righteousness, and all these things will be given to you as well."

(4) In **Luke 12:15** - "Then he said to them, "Watch out! Be on your guard against all kinds of greed; a man's life does not consist in the abundance of his possessions."

(5) In **Matthew 5:6** - "Blessed are those who hunger and thirst for righteousness, for they will be filled."

(6) In **Psalms 119:105** - " Your word is a lamp to my feet and a light for my path."

(7) In **Psalms 119:11** - " I have hidden your word in my heart that I might not sin against you."

(8) In **Matthew 22: 37-38** - " Jesus replied: " 'Love the Lord your God with all your heart and with all your soul and with all your mind. This is the first and greatest commandment."

(9) In **James 1:27** - "Religion that God our Father accepts as pure and faultless is this: to look after orphans and widows in their distress and to keep oneself from being polluted by the world. "

(10) In **Proverbs 8:17** - " I love those who love me, and those who seek me find me."

(11) In **2 Timothy 3:16-17** –"All Scripture is God-breathed and is useful for teaching, rebuking, correcting and training in righteousness, so that the man of God may be thoroughly equipped for every good work."

(12) In **Matthew 16: 24-26** - "Then said Jesus unto his disciples, if any man will come after me, let him deny himself, and take up his cross, and follow me. For whosoever will save his life shall lose it: and whosoever will lose his life for my sake shall find it. For what is a man profited, if he shall gain the whole world, and lose his own soul? Or what shall a man give in exchange for his soul?"

So in the end, mastering the ability to find balance in your life is a difficult challenge but one that will make a positive difference in your decision making ability.

As you consider how balanced your life is, I want to encourage you to take a step back and take a long, hard, look at your life. Evaluate your stress level, your priorities and answer the question of whether or not you are putting the Father first? Is your life self-centered or Christ-centered? Are you programmed to serve or are you looking first and foremost to be served?

As we have previously discussed, I believe the first step to restoring balance and living your life successfully is to seek His will, way, and word. Without the real peace of having a personal relationship with the Lord anchoring our lives and decisions, most of us will find ourselves feeling overwhelmed, stressed, unhappy, and lacking focus throughout the day. When we make the choice to lead a life of surrender and service, we are free to focus on what is really important and finish the day with a true sense of accomplishment, direction, and balance.

**Here are Eight (8) tips to Finding Balance In Life:**

1. **PUT GOD FIRST-** Christ must be at the center of everything. The Bible teaches us that our one and only priority is to keep Him, His Kingdom, and His righteousness first in everything. His will and our service to Him is our priority.

2. **Focus-** Be specific about the decisions, goals and objectives, which you establish.

3. **Take a Long Term View-** Make decisions in the present that can have the greatest positive impact on your future. Short- term decisions must align themselves with established long-term decisions.

4. **Take Responsibility -** You control your choices and are responsible for everything that happens and everything that you commit to.

5. **Limit Multi- tasking-** Performing several tasks less efficiently only serves to create anxiety, stress, and a sense of being out of control.

6. **Turn Off and Tune Out** – It is simply not possible or practical to believe that you can be "on" all 24/7/365. As the old saying reminds us, if you attempt to burn the candle from both ends you will either get burned or if successful run out of light twice as fast.

7. **Eliminate the Clutter-** Don't allow your life or your day to be or get too full.

8. **Plan-** Set clear priorities for each area of your life. Remember to always make the decision to choose the activities that will assure you the greatest health, happiness and financial success in the long term.

## Six (6) Questions to better Finding Balance In Life:

1. Would you say that in your life you possess: a) A lot of balance b) An average amount c) very little balance? What makes you think that?

2. When you think of the word "balance," as we're using it here, what thoughts come to your mind – overall, what are your attitudes about "balance"?

3. If you could change it, would you choose to have more balance in your life, or less? Why?

4. In what area of your life, right now, do you have the most balance? (Examples: This could be work, home, family, etc., or even attitudes, behaviors, habits, etc.)

5. In what area of your life, right now, do you have the least amount of balance?

6. If you wanted more balance in your life, what is one thing you could do, starting today, to achieve that?

Has your world ever been just rocked by some series of events?

Have you ever been motivated to really consider your priorities and life balance by the words of a loved one?

Have you come to these deep life questions perhaps by something that you watched or read?

Has any event in your life forced you into submission and an honest evaluation of life's fast track that you are on?

If so, I hope you will find solace in the fact that you aren't the first person to have experienced this and you won't be the last. If on the other hand you have not experienced these questions, you had better prepare for them, as it seems events happen to all of us that motivates these considerations.

The fact that we would get caught up like this shouldn't come as a surprise. After all, we are constantly bombarded by stimulus that encourages us to pour our lives into everything imaginable except that which is truly important. At every turn we are solicited, marketed, sold, and tempted to fill our lives with everything from making a million dollars in our spare time, to vacationing five times a year, to purchasing anything that we have ever dreamed of today, to the selling of our soul for a promotion. The list goes on and on. Keeping or maintaining balance in light of this all out assault on our time, dollar, and personal lifestyle is nearly impossible.

During this all out blitz period when our lives really seem to be lacking all balance, stop and spend a couple of hours providing a service that costs nothing except time to someone who needs you. I promise that your life will suddenly make sense again.

Consider these Five (5) Pitfalls to avoid to put you on the path to find balance in your life.

**Five (5) Life Balance Pitfalls to avoid:**

1) **Stress at Work** – One-fourth of employees rate their jobs as the number-one stressors in their lives.

2) **Financial Concern-** Money woes matter effecting and affecting every area of your life creating serious unbalance.

3) **Short Fuse** – If everything and everyone bothers you, more than likely the real issue that you are dealing with is that your lack of balance is draining your sense of humor, tolerance, and patience.

4) **Complicated Lifestyles** – Complicated lifestyles tend to be busy. Busy often causes stress. Stress causes your balance to get off center. To find balance and satisfaction in your life, simplify.

5) **Living by Default** – Don't allow your balance to be hijacked by others. Take back your life.

As a final thought on this subject, I would like you to consider that finding balance in your life is both energizing and liberating. It allows you to be who God intended you to be. In addition, when your life is balanced you are on the real path to great decision-making. To that end, it is important that you schedule a time each and everyday on your calendar for sufficient rest, exercise, relaxation and prayer if you seek to enjoy a healthy and balanced life.

**PRACTICE:** To practice the concept of balance this week, I'd like you to make a list in your Success Journal of three areas in which you would like to practice having more balance. Then write an action step for each one, telling yourself how you could accomplish that.

**PRAYER:** Heavenly Father all honor, praise and glory to you. Thank you for the many blessings that you have chosen to provide in my life. Father, all balance begins with placing you first in our lives. Your loving guidance provides us with the structure necessary for balance in our lives. The discipleship of discipline, which you instruct us, gives me strength and balance. Thank you Father for being my rock. I love you Lord.

*The Bible's training on fatherhood and parenting is not a testament to victimization or a short-term plan for happiness. It is the way.*

*It is the holy inspired word of our heavenly Father. It is the rulebook written by the God who not only wrote the book on love, relationship, and parenting but also created the game and established the rules of engagement.*

# CHAPTER TWELVE

## FATHERHOOD

**"When you teach your son, you teach your son's son"**

**The Talmud**

If I were a betting man, who I will admit that I am not, my bet would be that you are wondering what a chapter on Fatherhood is doing in a book about decision-making. Well in my humble opinion, one of the most important of many important decisions, which we will make in our lives, is to be a parent. From that point forward, each and every decision we make isn't only important but is critical. Our families view our priorities, abilities, skill set, and decisions as a measure of us as men, role models, and the leaders of our families. Each of our decisions shapes their processes, principles, values, morals, and ethics. Studies show that there is a direct correlation between how our children view us and how that shapes who they will become and what their relationship with the Father will be like.

Fatherhood is firmly rooted in Jesus, His word, way, and walk. It is this author's opinion that the Bible is without question the greatest book on parenting ever written. The Father's word has withstood thousands of years of scrutiny.

His principles and authority found in the Word are the same today as it was yesterday as it will be tomorrow. It is as relevant and true in today's world as it was 2000 years ago. It is the one set of truths that holds up against the test of time. It is not a fad. It is not new found or new age. It is not a here today and gone tomorrow self-help book. It is not a scrapbook of feel good theories that simply do not fair well when you exam their effectiveness and truths.

The life principles, provided for in the Bible, were not written as a part of some shell game, con, or get rich quick scheme. The Bible's training on fatherhood and parenting is not a testament to victimization or a short-term plan for happiness. It is the way.

It is the holy inspired word of our heavenly Father. It is the rulebook written by the God who not only wrote the book on love, relationship and parenting but also created the game and established the rules of engagement.

As a result, if you own the Bible, you need not spend another penny on any other parenting books. Reading and living the word will equip you to be a great parent and it will equip you to make decisions that make a real difference in the lives of those you touch and who trust you for guidance.

**Here is what the Lord has to say about Fatherhood in His word.**

(1) In **Proverbs 20:7** - "The righteous man leads a blameless life; blessed are his children after him."

(2) In **Malachi 4:6** - "He will turn the hearts of the fathers to their children, and the hearts of the children to their fathers; or else I will come and strike the land with a curse."

(3) In **Ephesians 6:4** - "Fathers, do not exasperate your children; instead, bring them up in the training and instruction of the Lord."

(4) In **Proverbs 22:6** - "Train a child in the way he should go, and when he is old he will not turn from it."

(5) In **1 Timothy 3:4** - "He must manage his own family well and see that his children obey him with proper respect."

(6) In **Hebrews 12:9** - "Moreover, we have all had human fathers who disciplined us and we respected them for it. How much more should we submit to the Father of our spirits and live!"

(7) In **Proverbs 19:13** - " A foolish son is his father's ruin, and a quarrelsome wife is like a constant dripping."

(8) In **Psalm 103:13** -  "As a father has compassion on his children, so the LORD has compassion on those who fear him"

(9) In **Colossians 3:2** - "Fathers, do not embitter your children, or they will become discouraged."

(10) In **1 Timothy 5:8** - "If anyone does not provide for his relatives, and especially for his immediate family, he has denied the faith and is worse than an unbeliever."

(11) In **Matthew 18:6** - "But if anyone causes one of these little ones who believe in me to sin, it would be better for

him to have a large millstone hung around his neck and to be drowned in the depths of the sea."

(12) In **Deuteronomy 6:6-9** - "These commandments that I give you today are to be upon your hearts. Impress them on your children. Talk about them when you sit at home and when you walk along the road, when you lie down and when you get up. Tie them as symbols on your hands and bind them on your foreheads. Write them on the doorframes of your houses and on your gates."

So in the end, you more than likely desire to be a father that makes a difference in your child's life. You probably desire to be a father whose children follow not out of fear, convenience, or because they have a void to fill, but rather because they trust, respect and love you. In the end, you hold to a heart felt desire to be a father whose lead is followed by his family because they know that you love them completely and have dedicated your life to them. In all these cases, consider the impact on the perception of your family when they see your relationship with Christ, your surrender, obedience, faithfulness, and prayer life. Consider the impact on them when your words and actions reflect salt and light.

Ask yourself whether you want to be secure in the knowledge that your family members have chosen to follow you out of their love, trust, and respect for you? Is it a long-term, top-level priority that your family's trust in you has resulted directly from the guidance, direction, and decision process that they have witnessed you employ? Are you willing to commit to never allowing yourself to break that trust relationship?

If you study the Bible, pray daily, and make decisions, which are Jesus driven, you and your family will have all the riches that the Lord has promised.

Remember that the Lord not only promises us but also took an oath on his promises. That is pretty impressive given that He is GOD and God doesn't lie. The Bible assures us that every word of God is flawless. You can live in complete confidence and have total faith and trust in the words, way, and walk of our Heavenly Father.

**Six (6) tips to successful Fatherhood:**

1) **Prepare your Heart-**It is God's will that the words written in His word jump out speaking loudly and clearly and make an impression on your hearts.

2) **Salt and Light-** That through the way we conduct God's business and live our lives daily, those looking to experience the love of our Lord will see his greatness and glory in our lives.

3) **Generation after Generation-**That by accepting God's gift of Jesus Christ and following his word, both your and your children's lives will be positively effected for generation upon generation.

4) **Blessings-**That your life will be richly blessed as a result of you becoming the father which Jesus has called upon and taught you to be.

5) **Live His Will-**That as an outgrowth of coming to know God's will, every aspect of every relationship you encounter will blossom.

6) **Seek His Promise-** That by finding and acting upon God's will right where you stand, you will find the peace, happiness and purpose that the Lord has promised and pledged to each of us.

Perhaps by this point, especially after studying scripture on the subject of fatherhood, you may agree with my contention that the Bible is the greatest book on parenting ever written. Actually, I would have no reluctance making the argument that the Bible is, in fact, the greatest book ever written on every life subject.

That aside, if we still don't agree on this one issue you shouldn't fault my effort. No harm, no foul. We can agree to disagree but I will keep trying. Even in the face of a disagreement on this point, the reality is that we should be able to come to agreement on the point that fatherhood is certainly one of the most consequential decisions a man will ever be in a position to make. In fact, there really can't be an argument that this one decision will result in and create an environment of thousands of ongoing critical decisions. Fatherhood may be the one decision you reach which causes literally a lifetime and in fact generations of critically important decisions.

### Six (6) Questions To A Successful Fatherhood:

1. Overall, how good a role model, leader, and father do you feel you are? a) Very good, b) good, c) Not as good as you'd like. Why do you feel that way?

2. How important do you think it is to be a world –class role model, leader, and father? (Why?)

3. When or in what situations, do you demonstrate making sound decisions most effectively?

4. When or in what situations, do you feel you demonstrate making sound decisions least effectively?

5. What one area of your fatherhood skills would you like to improve? (Why?)

6. If you could take one action, do one thing that would make you a more successfully role model, leader, father, husband, what would it be?

As a final thought on this subject, although most of us would like to believe otherwise, by the time we get married, start a career, and have a family more often than not we have not yet been blessed with a broad spectrum of wisdom, discernment, experience, or knowledge. As a result, if we are completely honest with ourselves, we can readily admit that we often make a habit of running around like a chicken with his head cut off, searching for happiness in all the wrong places. We seek it out in money, power, pleasure, recreation, possessions, and fame. Worst yet, we often convince ourselves that we seek these pleasures under the false premise that we are sacrificing for our families.

If we are honest with ourselves, we might just come to the realization that we are not sacrificing for our families but, in fact, sacrificing the future of our families. This may seem a harsh statement but unfortunately, more often, it ends up being a true statement.

The only question worth asking is whether our personal satisfaction is worth risking the long-term future of our families? Ask yourself whether or not you are willing to expose your family or your children to this life long risk for a shot at worldly possessions? How important and fulfilling are fame, fortune, pride, acceptance, and popularity for your ego or ambition? Do you realize that these short-term aphrodisiacs are all very fleeting… here today and gone tomorrow?

Making wise decisions on this subject will change your life for the positive. In the end, the good news is that you are only three (3) inches from being a world-class father.

Those three (3) inches represent my guess at the width of the average Bible.

So here is a chance to make a decision that will affect real answers, real solutions, and real results. All you have to do is invest the time, surrender, and serve the Lord and your Family. I trust that you will make the right decision.

**PRACTICE:** To practice the concept of fatherhood this week, I'd like you to make a list, in your Success Journal, of every selfless act, which you chose to undertake. Then for one week before every decision stop, wait, think about it, write it down and then deposit the money in a bank account for your children's education. Then, write down any instance when you made a decision that set an inappropriate example. Develop an action plan to avoid that behavior in the future.

**PRAYER:** Heavenly Father all honor, praise and glory to you. Your name is a mighty tower of strength and all who run to it are both safe and saved. Thank you for the many blessings that you have chosen to provide in my life. Father, you have blessed me with a family that looks to me for guidance and direction. Bless me with the discernment of character to teach them your word, will and way. Bless me with strength, faith, and love to put my self interest on the back burner and place their best interests in the fore front as you guide me in your will for them. Thank you Father for being my rock. I love you Lord.

*The decision to pray daily is a decision to get to know the Father more personally. It is a decision to look in the mirror each and everyday to reflect upon, evaluate, and adjust our walk. It is an opportunity to put our life in an order that is pleasing to the Father and rewarding for each of us.*

# CHAPTER THIRTEEN

## FAITHFULNESS IN PRAYER

**"Work as if you were to live a hundred years. Pray as if you were to die tomorrow."**

**Benjamin Franklin**

Faithfulness in prayer requires our constant diligence. The Bible calls us to be steadfastly attentive in prayer. When we pray without ceasing and give complete care and attention to prayer, we are following the will of God. We are pleasing our Father and causing Him joy.

The decision to pray daily is a decision to get to know the Father more personally. It is a decision to look in the mirror each and everyday to reflect upon, evaluate, and adjust our walk. It is an opportunity to put our life in an order that is pleasing to the Father and rewarding for each of us.

Our faithfulness encourages and allows God to disclose to and reward us greater insight than he chooses to expose to the less faithful. Faithfulness brings opportunities to us that are not revealed to the unfaithful. God takes great pleasure in answering prayers that comes from a faithful heart.

Your prayers reflect much about who you are, where you are in your life, and where you want to be. As Christians, we are encouraged to be persistent in our prayers. There is an abundance of evidence in the Bible to suggest that God rewards persistence. The Father wants to hear from us just as we want to hear from our children. The Father anxiously waits each and everyday for us to approach Him. He wants to have a personal relationship with each of us that is second to none.

He wants to move mountains for us. He desires to be there for us in times of trial and tribulation and to celebrate victories with us.

**Here is what the Lord has to say about Faithfulness In Prayer in His word.**

(1) In **Luke 2:36-38** - "There was also a prophetess, Anna, the daughter of Phanuel, of the tribe of Asher. She was very old; she had lived with her husband seven years after her marriage, and then was a widow until she was eighty-four. She never left the temple but worshiped night and day, fasting and praying. Coming up to them at that very moment, she gave thanks to God and spoke about the child to all who were looking forward to the redemption of Jerusalem.

(2) In **Romans 12:12** – "Be joyful in hope, patient in affliction, faithful in prayer."

(3) In **Romans 8:28** - "And we know that in all things God works for the good of those who love him, who have been called according to his purpose."

(4) In **Luke 18:1** - "Then Jesus told his disciples a parable to show them that they should always pray and not give up. Therefore I remind you to stir up the gift of God which is in you through the laying on of my hands."

Our faithfulness in prayer will in fact reap large rewards. Luke instructs us that "Whoever can be trusted with very little can also be trusted with much, and whoever is dishonest with very little will also be dishonest with much."

To those who set time aside each day to be faithful in prayer, God leads us into a deeper relationship trusting more responsibilities to us. Each time the Father reveals more to us and we are faithful with that blessing He provides to us, He has confidence to give us more to handle.

A decision on our part to set aside time each day to demonstrate our faithfulness in prayer, directly leads to our ability to attain a higher call, which links directly to our success, happiness, and peace.

**Here are Six (6) tips to increase Your Faithfulness In Prayer:**

1. **PUT GOD FIRST-** Christ must be at the center of everything. The Bible teaches us that our one and only priority is to keep Him, His Kingdom, and His righteousness first in everything. His will and our service to Him is our priority.

2. **Pray Daily-** The Lord Instructed Us to Pray. The best reason to spend time in prayer is because the Lord instructed us to.

3. **Develop a Daily Devotional Plan** –Decide on a time, place, general structure, and spend time in prayer, petition, praise, and worship.

4. **Pray Persistently** - Continue persisting in your prayers. It is prayer, which strengthens our faith, providing us hope and assurance.

5. **Fight Discouragement** – We are instructed to "walk by faith and not by sight." Regardless of how we see things turning out, we should continue to devote ourselves to prayer. In the place of discouragement, we must have faith in all things and faith that everything will turn out for the good.

6. **Pray For Others** - God is looking for intercessors that are willing to continue to pray and to believe until they see God's answer.

**Six (6) Questions To increase Your Faithfulness In Prayer:**

1. Are you willing to move forward in you prayer life, on faith, or do you have to know where you're going before you get there?   Why?

2. In the past, has your "faith" in something you wanted to accomplish, usually work, or not?  Why do you think that is? Did you pray over it?

3. Are you typically willing to: a) Have a lot of faith in your ideas, b) Sometimes have faith in your ideas, or c) Almost never have faith in your ideas? Do you pray for the Father's will or for Him to bless your will?

4. Do you have a regular prayer life?  (How strong is it?)

5. If you wanted to have an incredible amount of faith in something you really wanted to achieve, would you faithfully pray to achieve it?

6. In addition to prayer what is the one thing you could do, right now, to have more faith in whom you are, and what you want to do most?

In **Luke 2:36-38** we are introduced to Anna. Anna had been a widow for many years. Anna spent her time, day and night, in prayer and fasting in the temple. She prayed faithfully of her desire to see the Son of God. Anna was one of the very few that God chose to encounter the Savior when He was born. Jesus was only revealed to those whose hearts were faithful and pure. Anna had such a heart.

So in the end, we know that Anna continued faithfully in prayer until her prayer was answered. The answer to her prayer did not come immediately. In fact, it came near the end of her life. It took nearly sixty years for Anna's prayer to be answered. During those sixty years, she was a widow who had no family, no financial resources, no rights, no home, no assets and no legacy but what she did have was faithful prayer. Clearly with the Lord, that is all that matters.

Consider all that she didn't have but God still found it important to honor what she did have, that being her faithfulness. Anna was ultimately honored and privileged to be the one chosen to announce the arrival of the Savior to those in the Temple.

What an incredible and awesome answer, honor and reward for her faithfulness.

As a final thought on this subject, as it was for Anna, faithful praying may mean a lifetime of waiting to receive an answer. God is looking for intercessors, like Anna, that are willing to continue to faithfully pray on His answer for however long it may take.

**PRACTICE:** To practice the concept of faith this week, I'd like you to practice having faith – in everything you'd like to achieve or accomplish, all week long. Then, make a list of the things you decided to have faith in, and write down what worked and what didn't. Remember, the more faith you choose to have, the better things work! Also, try setting time aside and faithfully use that time each day for prayer.

**PRAYER:** Heavenly Father all honor, praise and glory to you. Thank you for the many blessings that you have chosen to provide in my life. Father, in **Romans 12:12** your advice could not be any clearer as we are instructed **"Be joyful in hope, patient in affliction, faithful in prayer."** I come to you in petition asking that you give me the boldness to honor and obey your command. Thank you Father for being here for me. I love you Lord.

*At its base level the reality is that the Revolutionary mind-set is simple: Make whatever decisions, take whatever steps and actions necessary to enhance our relationship with our heavenly Father and then be willing, anxious, and available to help others do the same.*

# CHAPTER FOURTEEN

## THE REVOLUTION

**"Every generation needs a new revolution"**

**Thomas Jefferson**

Does the title of this article invoke images of The Minutemen and our country's battle for independence? How about Marxists, Communists, Socialists, Sandinistas, or the Taliban?

The Beatles had a hit song Revolution that opened "You say you want a revolution; well, you know; we all want to change the world." Good song, but I am not referring to it, although it is a catchy tune and we might revisit the lyrics again a bit later.

So we have established that the title reference isn't to a hit song. It most certainly isn't to any leader or group espousing a particular Worldly movement. Than to what type of Revolution are we referring?

Well here's a hint. The Revolution is not a reference to a violent revolution but one of the peace and love that Jesus Christ demonstrated to us in his word, way, walk and life.

My hope is that the title may, in fact, be a reference to you, my Christian brothers or sisters.

**Let's find out if you are an active member of the Revolution.**

1) Do you believe that every word of the Bible is flawless and is God's authentic, true and reliable Word for life?

2) Do you believe that the meaning of life can be found in surrender and service?

3) Do you honestly pursue a personal and intimate relationship with our Father each and everyday?

4) Do you believe that you either live your life for Jesus or by definition your life reflects all that He died to reject and save us from?

5) Do you turn to God's Word the Bible for answers, solutions, guidance, and direction?

6) Do you live only to love, obey, and serve the Father?

7) Do you evaluate every decision, opportunity, and obstacle in light of Jesus' Word, Way, and Walk?

8) Do you worship God everyday, both in private and in the company of other believers?

9) Do you place your faith at the center of your life gaining all sense of purpose, direction, and meaning from that personal relationship?

10)Do you love the Lord your God with all your heart and with all your soul, with your entire mind and with all your strength?

Unlike most of the tests that life presents us with, this little ten-question test isn't pass or fail. There isn't a Bell curve to come to your aid and save your grade. You can't move on to the next level with little work, minimal effort, and unenthusiastic passing grades. No, this test requires 100% commitment followed up by constant re-commitment to the pursuit of His excellence.

At its base level the reality is that the Revolutionary mind-set is simple: Make whatever decisions, take whatever steps and actions necessary to enhance our relationship with our heavenly Father and then be willing, anxious, and available to help others do the same.

To successfully accomplish this goal, we must always be conscious that the proof of our faith is not found in the vast amount of knowledge and information, which we have memorized. It is not found in whom we know, or are known to hang out with, or who is in our social circles. It is not found in or based upon the religious events we attend. It's not found in how much we contribute/donate so that others can serve on our behalf. It isn't about what we aspire to have our legacy be within our community.

It is found where the rubber hits the road. It is found in the way you partner what you know and what you believe into everyday practices. It is found when your profession of faith in Christ is supported by a lifestyle, decision process, and heart that provide indisputable evidence of your Christ-centeredness and complete devotion to Jesus. It is found when you constantly seek and obey His will. It is found in surrender and service. It is found in your heart.

**Here are ten (10) truths that the Lord has to say about Your Role In The Revolution in His word.**

(1) In **Romans 1:16** –" I am not ashamed of the gospel, because it is the power of God for the salvation of everyone who believes: first for the Jew, then for the Gentile."

(2) In **Matthew 6:33** - "But seek first his kingdom and his righteousness, and all these things will be given to you as well."

(3) In **Romans13: 11** "And do this, understanding the present time. The hour has come for you to wake up from your slumber, because our salvation is nearer now than when we first believed."

(4) In **1 John 4:15** - "Whoever confesses that Jesus is the Son of God, God abides in him, and he in God." 1 Thessalonians 5:4-5 – "But you, brothers, are not in darkness so that this day should surprise you like a thief. You are all sons of the light and sons of the day. We do not belong to the night or to the darkness."

(5) In **John 12:25** "The man who loves his life will lose it, while the man who hates his life in this world will keep it for eternal life."

(6) In **Ephesians 5:14** - "for the light makes everything visible. This is why it is said, "Awake, O sleeper, rise up from the dead, and Christ will give you light."

(7) In **Mark 16:15** - "And he said to them, "Go into all the world and preach the gospel to all creation."

(8) In **Matthew 7:7-11** - "Ask and it will be given to you; seek and you will find; knock and the door will be opened to you. For everyone who asks receives; he who seeks finds; and to him who knocks, the door will be opened."

(9) In **2 Timothy 4:2** - "Preach the word; be ready in season and out of season; reprove, rebuke, exhort, with great patience and instruction."

(10) In **John 14:6** – " Jesus answered, "I am the way and the truth and the life. No one comes to the Father except through me."

**Here are Eight (8) tips to be a part of The Christ Lead Revolution:**

1. **Be A Revolutionary** –At all times lead and live your life in total surrender, complete obedience and always seeking His will.

2. **Live To Honor Jesus** - Evaluate all decisions, actions, and feelings in light of what the Bible teaches us.

3. **Daily Worship, Praise, and Prayer** - It is a loving and intimate expression of a grateful, loving, obedient heart that has encountered the Holy Spirit. How priceless God's gift of salvation is?

4. **Practice Christ-centeredness** - Place your faith in the center of your life, your beliefs, and your actions.

5. **Surrender Completely** - Love your Father and trust Him without reservation.

6. **Serve Your neighbor** - Servant hood demonstrates the truth of God's unfailing love to those who feel, experience, and witness it. In the words of Isaiah, "Here am I. Send me!"

7. **Follow Faithfully** – Faith keeps us in a trusting relationship with God. Nothing is more secure or certain than that which we entrust to God.

8. **Commit Totally** – You can't be a part time disciple and please your maker.

So in the end, "You say you want a revolution." To be a true revolutionary, a prayer warrior, and a Kingdom builder it is not sufficient that you just faithfully go to church. You have to be willing to become the church in way, walk, and word. You must be prepared to commit 100% of yourself to being Salt and Light. You have to commit your life to living to serve, not being served.

"You say you want a revolution; well, you know; we all want to change the world." Great stuff! Fortunately, the truth is that every one of us is blessed with special gifts and talents that could be utilized to make the world a better place in which to live. In the event that your skill(s) was previously hidden or dormant, now is the time to take advantage and pursue them in the name of the Father.

As a final thought on this subject, if you want to be part of His revolution ask yourself the question. In whose life did I make a difference today? In fact, reflect upon that question many times each day.

**PRAYER:** Heavenly Father all honor, praise and glory to you. Thank you, and please accept the offering of my life to you. Allow me the honor of being one of those chosen to be a part of your revolution. Bless me with the courage and boldness to be a warrior for your life. Allow me to live a life of salt and light so that all who see me know me to be of the Spirit. Thank you Father for being my rock. I love you Lord.

*So, in the end, it seems apparent that the Father anticipants that we will consider His signs to us as directive and His expectation is that we will come to him prayerfully seeking the Father's will and obediently following His way, word, and walk.*

*In this regard, the true rationale for signs in our life can only be found in the search for and the achievement of the purposes for which God created us. That is ultimately what will make us happy and insure our thirst and quest for direction, purpose, and success in our desire to render Christ like decisions.*

# CHAPTER FIFTEEN

## CAN YOU SEE THE SIGNS?

But whoever catches a glimpse of the revealed counsel of God—the free life! —Even out of the corner of his eye, and sticks with it, is no distracted scatterbrain but a man or woman of action. That person will find delight and affirmation in the action.

### James 1:19-27 (The Message)

Have you ever experienced having a song from your past that mysteriously and annoyingly played over and over again in your head?

When that happens, how do you handle it? Do you consider whether or not there is some reason why this particular song

Len Stubbs

happened to appear out of nowhere and decide to taunt you?

This was recently the situation that I found myself in when out of nowhere and for no apparent reason, this one oldie but goody kept entering my psyche. It happened with the song "Signs" that greatly popularized the somewhat unknown Canadian rock group, Five Man Electrical Band, who wrote and performed it in 1971. For those of you old enough, you may remember that "Signs" was fairly popular having reached number three on the Billboard charts.

The chorus of the song has the following lyrics:

"Sign, sign, everywhere a sign. Blocking out the scenery, breaking my mind. Do this, don't do that, can't you read the sign?"

In the last set of verses despite not having any money to contribute to the collection, the singer is accepted in a Christian church worship service, where he decides to write his own sign to the Father. His choice to send this message to the Father is an acknowledgement that when seemingly all around you others are exclusionary, the Father accepts you, unconditionally, regardless of lifestyle, financial standing, etc.

In that verse are the following lyrics:

And the sign said, "Everybody welcome, come in, kneel down, and pray. "And when they passed around the plate at the end of it all, I didn't have a penny to pay. So I got me a pen and a paper and I made up my own little sign, I said, "Thank you, Lord, for thinking about me, I'm alive and doing fine."

Believe it or not, but I went around with this song in my head for a few weeks until the message that this sign was conveying hit me like a ton of bricks. It became clear to me that in our Christian walk the Lord directs us each day, all day with His will for us. He provides us signs as to his will, plan, and purpose for each of us, we just have to learn how to pay attention to it.

As a Christ-centered man seeking the Father's will, this should have been self-evident. Unfortunately, although I actually spent time with the Lord on it's meaning, the message the sign was conveying was not quickly apparent.

A difficult, yet important life lesson for most of us to learn is that if you aren't actively seeking the signs when you first see them, it is often difficult to recognize them as a sign or direction.

There is an old adage that seems appropriate here. It goes something like... if you are not consciously seeking a direction for your life, any map will do, since it doesn't really matter where you end up.

In Matthew 2:1-12 we learn of the visit of the magi: After Jesus was born in Bethlehem in Judea, during the time of King Herod, Magi from the east came to Jerusalem and asked, "Where is the one who has been born king of the Jews? We saw his star in the east and have come to worship him."

"When King Herod heard this he was disturbed, and all Jerusalem with him. When he had called together all the people's chief priests and teachers of the law, he asked them where the Christ was to be born. "In Bethlehem in Judea," they replied, "for this is what the prophet has written:" 'But you, Bethlehem, in the land of Judah, are by no means least among the rulers of Judah; for out of you will come a ruler who will be the shepherd of my people Israel.'

Then Herod called the Magi secretly and found out from them the exact time the star had appeared. He sent them to Bethlehem and said, "Go and make a careful search for the child. As soon as you find him, report to me, so that I too may go and worship him."

After they had heard the king, they went on their way, and the star they had seen in the east went ahead of them until it stopped over the place where the child was. When they saw the star, they were overjoyed. On coming to the house, they saw the child with his mother Mary, and they bowed down and worshiped him. Then they opened their treasures and presented him with gifts of gold and of incense and of myrrh. And having been warned in a dream not to go back to Herod, they returned to their country by another route."

In this story of Christ's birth, we know that there was a sign, a star in the east. What we don't know is why some could see it and comprehend it's significant (the wise men) and some couldn't (Herod). The wise men knew to give all honor, praise, glory, and worship to the baby Christ. Herod, as we know, wanted to kill him.

Which brings us to the second sign spoken in these twelve verses of scripture. The wise men having been warned in a dream not to go back to Herod returned to their country by another route.

Do you find it interesting that in the same story, just twelve verses in this one passage, that the Father demonstrates to us a sign which is a wonder (the star), and a sign that is an ordinary event (dream). Both signs, both significant and both representing the difference between walking by sight and walking by faith.

The evidence and signs of God's presence whether in signs, in wonders, in resurrection, in nature, or in the natural day to day flow of our lives, will be seen by some while never seen by others. It is curious that for some in attendance seeing water turned into wine before their very eyes wasn't significant as they remained blind to what had happened.

A Newsweek poll indicated that 84% of Americans say they believe God performs miracles/ wonders/signs; 48% claim to have experienced or witnessed one. What do you believe?

An answer to this query can be found exactly where you would expect to find it, in scripture. Jesus teaches us about two kinds of sight: physical and spiritual, the sight of the eyes and the sight of the heart. The one is common to all who look; the Holy Spirit must reveal the other. While the evidence of God's hand in the ordinary may be obvious, sometimes overwhelming, if we are to experience even a small part of the revelation that filled Jesus with such joy, we must be given eyes of faith, a heart to see, and a passion for obedience.

**Here are six (6) reasons Why God generally uses signs in our midst:**

1. Signs serve as a confirmation of a person's ministry or message.

    A. The minister (person) that he is sent by God.

    B. The message (word) that it is from God.

2. In the Old Testament, signs or wonders served as evidence of the one true God.

3. God performs signs to meet the needs of His people.

4. Signs increase our faith.

5. God sends them sometimes as judgment upon the unjust.

6. They may simply be symbolic in nature.

**Here is what the Lord has to say about Signs in His word.**

(1) In **James 1:25** – But whoever catches a glimpse of the revealed counsel of God—the free life! —Even out of

the corner of his eye, and sticks with it, is no distracted scatterbrain but a man or woman of action. That person will find delight and affirmation in the action.

(2) In **Acts 4:30** - Stretch out your hand to heal and perform miraculous signs and wonders through the name of your holy servant Jesus."

(3) In **Matthew 16:8-10** - Aware of their discussion, Jesus asked, "You of little faith, why are you talking among yourselves about having no bread? Do you still not understand? Don't you remember the five loaves for the five thousand, and how many basketfuls you gathered? Or the seven loaves for the four thousand, and how many basketfuls you gathered?

(4) In **John 6:16-21** - When evening came, his disciples went down to the lake, where they got into a boat and set off across the lake for Capernaum. By now it was dark, and Jesus had not yet joined them. A strong wind was blowing and the waters grew rough. When they had rowed three or three and a half miles, they saw Jesus approaching the boat, walking on the water; and they were terrified. But he said to them, "It is I; don't be afraid." Then they were willing to take him into the boat, and immediately the boat reached the shore where they were heading.

(5) In **John 12:9** - Meanwhile a large crowd of Jews found out that Jesus was there and came, not only because of him but also to see Lazarus, whom he had raised from the dead.

(6) In **John 20:30** - Jesus did many other miraculous signs in the presence of his disciples, which are not recorded in this book.

(7) In **Luke 9:12-17** - Late in the afternoon the Twelve came to him and said, "Send the crowd away so they can go

to the surrounding villages and countryside and find food and lodging, because we are in a remote place here. "He replied, "You give them something to eat. "They answered, "We have only five loaves of bread and two fish—unless we go and buy food for all this crowd." (About five thousand men were there.) But he said to his disciples, "Have them sit down in groups of about fifty each." The disciples did so, and everybody sat down. Taking the five loaves and the two fish and looking up to heaven, he gave thanks and broke them. Then he gave them to the disciples to set before the people. They all ate and were satisfied, and the disciples picked up twelve basketfuls of broken pieces that were left over.

(8) In **Mark 6:45-52** - Immediately Jesus made his disciples get into the boat and go on ahead of him to Bethsaida, while he dismissed the crowd. After leaving them, he went up on a mountainside to pray. When evening came, the boat was in the middle of the lake, and he was alone on land. He saw the disciples straining at the oars, because the wind was against them. About the fourth watch of the night he went out to them, walking on the lake. He was about to pass by them, but when they saw him walking on the lake, they thought he was a ghost. They cried out, because they all saw him and were terrified. Immediately he spoke to them and said, "Take courage! It is I. Don't be afraid." Then he climbed into the boat with them, and the wind died down. They were completely amazed, for they had not understood about the loaves; their hearts were hardened.

(9) In **Mark 11:12-14** - The next day as they were leaving Bethany, Jesus was hungry. Seeing in the distance a fig tree in leaf, he went to find out if it had any fruit. When he reached it, he found nothing but leaves, because it was not the season for figs. Then he said to the tree, "May no one ever eat fruit from you again." And his disciples heard him say it.

The Bible is clear that for most of us, signs are a form of education, communication, direction, and are important. Scripture teaches us that by the time Jesus called Lazarus back to life, He was drawing large crowds of both faithful and skeptical followers wherever he traveled. Some of the followers where driven to follow Jesus primarily because of the signs and wonders, while others followed because of faith and trust which the signs blessed.

We know that as an outward sign for all to witness, Jesus gave the twelve powers over demons and to heal diseases. God has given to every believer the power to perform the same mighty deeds as Jesus Himself did, if we have faith.

While all believers have been given this blessing, we are instructed that along with this power comes responsibility. In this case, the responsibility is faith, trust, and humility. We are instructed that no matter who is the vessel God uses to bring about a sign or healing, it is God who is to receive the glory for it. When Paul healed the cripple at Lystra and the people all cried, "The gods are come down to us ... " he rebuked them for thinking it was by his own power that it had been done.

In Luke 10:21-24, we are instructed that Jesus, full of joy through the Holy Spirit, said, "I praise you, Father, Lord of heaven and earth, because you have hidden these things from the wise and learned, and revealed them to little children. Yes, Father, for this was your good pleasure. "All things have been committed to me by my Father. No one knows who the Son is except the Father, and no one knows who the Father is except the Son and those to whom the Son chooses to reveal him. "Then he turned to his disciples and said privately, "Blessed are the eyes that see what you see. For I tell you that many prophets and kings wanted to see what you see but did not see it, and to hear what you hear but did not hear it."

We are taught that although Jesus on occasion uses signs to get our attention, that as our personal relationship with the

Father grows faith, obedience, and grace are sufficient to get our attention.

This first sign that scripture speaks to is Jesus turning water into wine. As miraculous as it is, the more important point is that it serves to make the case that signs are not about tricks or miracles but rather focus us on the truth that Jesus Is glory, truth, and love. Signs like these in scripture teach us and reflect the truth that Jesus is capable of controlling all creation because he is the Son of God. As the one and only son Jesus is all-powerful. Yes, these signs were the miracles of Jesus, healing the blind and sick, walking on the water, feeding thousands of people with a few loaves of bread and a small number of fish, bringing Lazarus back to life after death, freeing people from being possessed by demons, arranging for a net out in the waters to be made completely full of fish. These miracles were signs in the sense that they are meant to direct us to Jesus, who He is in our lives, and to grow in our understanding of our relationship with Him.

In Luke 11:27-28, "As Jesus was saying these things, a woman in the crowd called out, "Blessed is the mother who gave you birth and nursed you." Jesus replied, "Blessed rather are those who hear the word of God and obey it."

Having created us, Jesus knows our heart all too well. As such, He cautions us that in the visible world, a sign represents a tangible experience on which to grasp to understand His power, glory, forgiveness, and eternal love.

He is well aware that his children are easily impressed with the spectacular. Scripture says that the crowds in Jesus' day "marveled" and were "greatly astonished" at the things done in their midst.

The truth is that many followed Him because they had seen the signs He had performed. Still others said they would not believe except if they saw a sign. Some even despite the signs done in their midst, still refused to repent and believe. While others, we are told, are unable to recognize the sign.

The Father doesn't want us to be focused upon and devoted to the show. He cautions us not to be consumed only by the demonstrable signs and wonders while missing the real glory of the heavenly God.

The old saying about seeing the forest for the trees is applicable here.

Scripture instructs us that we are not to seek a sign (Matthew 12:38-39; 16:4). In its place, we are taught that the signs are to follow us (Mark 16:17), not we the signs. The closer your walk and the more mature your relationship with the Father, the more driven and focused you will be to seek His will in all things. The more focused that you are on being obedient to the Father's call, the more likely you are to recognize the signs, communication, and direction he provides.

In the end, it is through faith that we must come to accept Jesus' teachings, love, and forgiveness. We are instructed that some will be given to see and from others the same knowledge would be hidden? This was the case with Herod, as he was not blessed to discern the sign, for we know that not all have eyes that see and ears that hear. Signs can be as routine as a blade of grass, a star in the heavens, a sunrise, or as wondrous as the Father sending His son, Jesus to be crucified, die on a cross, and be resurrected.

The Holy Spirit calls us to faith but Jesus recognizes the value of the sign for those who need a little push. Today's Christian believer is called to respond to signs in our life with the same reaction that scripture tells us that the crowds of Jesus' day responded. We are called to celebrate them with worship, prayer, devotion, and thankfulness.

**A sign is the occurrence of any event apparently contra-dictory to and unexplainable by the laws of science, and usually attributed to God**:

While many signs and wonders occurred in the time of the Old Testament the greatest sign was delivered in the New Testament that of course being the virgin birth, life, and cross of our Savior Jesus Christ.

## SIGNS FROM THE OLD TESTAMENT:

1. The sun stood still at Joshua's command.

2. Water flowed from a rock when Moses struck it.

3. The Red Sea parted so that God's people could cross.

4. An iron ax floated on water

5. The waters were turned to blood.

6. The dead were raised to life.

    A. The son of the widow of Zarephath.

    B. The Shunammite's son

    The young man laid in Elisha's sepulcher

7. Aaron 's rod blossomed

8. The three Hebrew children in the fiery furnace remained unharmed

9. The widow's cruse of oil and barrel of meal was continually replenished during a time of famine.

10. Baalam's ass spoke.

11. Jonah, swallowed by a whale, was vomited up alive after three days in its belly.

12. Moses' rod became a serpent; his hand became temporarily leprous when he put his hand in his bosom.

13. The Jordan parted when Elijah "smote the waters" with his mantle.

14. The sun went backwards.

15. Manna fell from the sky to feed God's people.

16. Gideon's fleece became wet and dry according to his request concerning the word of the Lord to him.

17. Elijah pronounced a drought upon the land, "and it rained not on the earth by the space of three years and six months. And he prayed again, and the heaven gave rain ... "

**Jesus Himself performed many mighty signs and wonders among the people:**

1.  He changed water into wine

2.  He walked on water.

3.  He took money from the mouth of a fish.

4.  He fed the multitudes with a few loaves and fishes.

     A. The five thousand

     B. The four thousand.

5.  He cursed a fig tree, and it shriveled up.

6.  He told the storm to cease, and it became silent.

7.  At His word the dead were raised to life.

    A. The widow's son

    B. Jairus' daughter.

    C. Lazarus.

8.  At His command his disciples brought in a draught of fish where there had been none.

**The early church experienced many miracles as well:**

1.  Those bitten by poisonous snakes remained

2.  Those imprisoned for the gospel's sake escaped unharmed.

3.  Those upon whom just the shadow of Peter fell were made whole.

4.  "And God wrought special miracles by the hands of Paul, so that from his body were brought unto the sick handkerchiefs or aprons, and the diseases departed from them, and the evil spirits went out of them."

5.  The dead were raised to life.

    A. Peter raised Dorcas (Tabitha).

    B. Paul raised Eutychus

It is important to recognize that Satan can also perform lying signs and wonders. Remember that not everything supernatural is of God.

The Holy Spirit has provided for the gift of miracles in the church. The basic element necessary to operate in this realm of ministry is faith. In the last days, power will be given the two witnesses "to shut heaven, that it rain not in the days of their prophecy," and to turn waters "to blood, and to smite the earth with all plagues, as often as they will."

Have you not known? Have you not heard? Asks Isaiah. Those with ears to hear, let them hear, says Jesus. Day to day pours forth speech, says the psalmist, but God's speech is pitched in such a register that many cannot distinguish it from silence. Each of us is called to master the discipline of stillness. Stillness that is critical, as it allows the Lord to reflect a little piece of His heart on ours.

In the sacraments, we strain to recognize a divine word, even if it has to be mediated through the preacher's voice. At the baptismal waters, parents hear how the heavens opened above Jesus, the Spirit of God descended on him in the form of a dove, and a voice spoke from heaven, saying, "This is my beloved child, with whom I am well pleased." They hear this readily because they too are well pleased with their children and have come to hear this love ratified.

### Six (6) Questions to understanding Why Signs:

## Do you ever feel, like asking Jesus?

1. "Who are you"? Why do I feel a need to know you?

2. Who are you in my life? What role do I play in your plan?

3. How am I to relate to you? When will we be together?

4. What am I to believe about you? How do I ascertain your will from my will?

5. What am I to think, feel, and do when it comes to me understanding my relationship with you?" What is Christ-centered obedience?

6. How do I broaden my perspective and focus every day on growing our personal relationship?

If you are a baseball fan perhaps this analogy will make sense. Prior to each game and in fact often several times during the game the team manager communicates team signs and changes to team signs to his staff and players. Even though the opposing manager, coaching staff, players, and in fact all in attendance can see the coaches giving his batters, base runners, and pitchers these signs more often than not none of these witnesses have any idea what is the meaning, direction, or intended communications behind the sign that the coach is offering.

In this example consider the Father the manager and those of us looking for a sign and knowing what to look for the hitters at the plate. After each pitch we look to the Manager who signals us to take, bunt, steal, hit and run or hit away. Although many are present to witness the sign very few recognize its instructive message. Those who do recognize have a different set of options and opportunities at their disposal. As the players at bat and witnesses to the sign we have the option to be obedient to the direction and will of the manager or to act on our own accord based upon our own instincts. Most of us knowing the consequence of failure to obey and recognizing that the manager understands the big picture follow his lead, direction, and instruction.

So, in the end, it seems apparent that the Father anticipants that we will consider His signs to us as directive and His expectation is that we will come to him prayerfully seeking the Father's will and obediently following His way, word, and walk.

In this regard, the true rationale for signs in our life can only be found in the search for and the achievement of the purposes for which God created us. That is ultimately what will make us happy and insure both our thirst and quest for direction, purpose, and success in our desire to render Christ like decisions.

**PRACTICE:** To practice your perception of signs this week, I'd like you to start each morning by asking yourself two questions: 1. "What surrounds me that I see virtually everyday that when I slow down I recognize as being of the creator?" 2. " Upon reflection what has happened recently that I originally viewed as a coincidence that upon second thought may well be a sign from the Father?" (Be sure to write your thoughts and ideas on "recognizing signs," in your Success Journal.)

**PRAYER:** Heavenly Father all honor, praise and glory to you. Thank you for the many blessings that you have chosen to provide in my life. Father, what an honor it is to know that you wait patiently each day for our time together. I come to you at this point seeking discernment as to your will for my life. Please continue to communicate direction to me through your word, spirit, and signs.

Father please accept my oath that as you direct my actions that I will be faithfully obedient.

Lord I know that when I align my life to your will that my life will be blessed with success. Thank you Father for being here for me. I love you Lord.

*Then he said, "Do you understand what I have done to you? You address me as 'Teacher' and 'Master,' and rightly so. That is what I am. So if I, the Master and Teacher, washed your feet, you must now wash each other's feet. I've laid down a pattern for you. What I've done, you do. I'm only pointing out the obvious. A servant is not ranked above his master; an employee doesn't give orders to the employer. If you understand what I'm telling you, act like it—and live a blessed life."*

# CHAPTER SIXTEEN

## FOLLOW ME

**"Don't follow me, follow Jesus!"**

**"Exercise daily - walk with God."**

After all these pages we finally get to the most important decision that you will ever make in your entire life. Not just the most important decision for you personally but truly the most important decision that you will ever make in the lives of those you love. Not to place any pressure on you or anything but this is a decision that affects not only your life span but also effects multiple generations of your family. Other than that it is really no big deal.

As a result of the high stakes involved if you choose to reread any chapter, please reread this chapter as many times as it takes for you to surrender to your calling from the Father to "Follow Me".

At the beginning of His ministry Jesus called the first disciples. After fervently praying with the Father over this selection process, Jesus was walking beside the Sea of Galilee. As he knew he would, he came upon two brothers, Simon (later called Peter) and Andrew. They were throwing their nets into the lake, for they were fishermen by trade. "Come, follow me," Jesus said, "and I will make a new kind of fisherman out of you. I will make you fishers of men; I will show you how to catch men and women instead of perch and bass." At once, immediately without question or discussion their decision was to obediently leave both their nets and business to follow Him.

Going on from there, a short distance down the beach Jesus came upon another pair of brothers, James and John, Zebedee's sons.

These two were sitting in a boat with their father, Zebedee, mending their fishnets. Jesus called out to them making the same offer, which He earlier had made to Peter and Andrew, and they were just as quick to follow, abandoning boat and father to follow Him.

They didn't ask questions or consider the options they simply dropped their nets and obediently followed.

Do you think that it is revealing that Jesus started out His ministry, following spending time with the Father in prayer, asking His disciples to Follow Me? Do you think that it is revealing that those He selected to Follow Him obediently aligned their life to His will and Followed Him?

Let me fast forward to the Last Supper it was just before the Passover Feast, Jesus knew that the time had come to leave this world to return home to the Father. Having loved his disciples, he now showed them the full extent of his love. He continued to love and equip them right to the end.

It was suppertime, the evening meal was being served, and the devil now had Judas, son of Simon the Iscariot, firmly in his grip, and had already prompted him to betray Jesus.

Jesus knew that the Father had put him in complete charge of everything and all things under his power. He was well aware that He had come from God and was returning to God. To further equip His chosen associates, he got up from the supper table and His meal, took off his outer clothing, setting aside his robe, and wrapped a towel around his waist. He then poured water into a basin and began to wash the feet of the disciples, drying them with his apron. When he got to Simon Peter, Peter said, "Master, you wash my feet?"

Jesus answered, "You don't understand now what I'm doing, but it will be clear enough to you later."

Let me stop here and clarify that at the time of Jesus no one aspired to be a slave. Trust me when I say that no one wanted to be the slave that washed feet. For this was a role assigned to the lowest of lowly slaves. In the slave world slaves looked down on the foot washing slave as less than worthy.

As a point of history back in the day foot washing was traditionally observed before feasts and banquets. In the dry dusty Middle East, feet that were sandaled quickly got rough looking. The guests having washed, cleaned and gotten them all gussied up for the gathering would only need their feet washed to be presentable to their hosts.

The disciples were no different they had properly prepared themselves for the evenings festivities. However there was no servant available for foot washing. Just a coincidence I guess.

The disciples being at a supper wanted to be served not serve and they most certainly were not willing to volunteer as the replacement foot-washing slave.

What do you think their reaction was when Jesus the Master chose to become the lowest of lowly slaves, a foot washer?

After he had finished washing their feet, he took his robe, put it back on, and went back to his place at the table.

Then he said, "Do you understand what I have done to you? You address me as 'Teacher' and 'Master,' and rightly so. That is what I am. So if I, the Master and Teacher, washed your feet, you must now wash each other's feet. I've laid down a pattern for you. What I've done, you do. I'm only pointing out the obvious.

A servant is not ranked above his master; an employee doesn't give orders to the employer. If you understand what I'm telling you, act like it—and live a blessed life.

In other words Jesus told His disciples to follow me, follow my example of humble service. Cause the Father joy by surrender, obedience, service and love for our neighbor. Jesus makes no bones about it…. follow me and you will be blessed if you live the life that I have equipped you to live.

Here is what the Lord has to say about **Follow Me** in His word.

(1) In **John 12:24-26** - "I tell you the truth, unless a kernel of wheat falls to the ground and dies, it remains only a single seed. But if it dies, it produces many seeds. The man who loves his life will lose it, while the man who hates his life in this world will keep it for eternal life. Whoever serves me must follow me; and where I am, my servant also will be. My Father will honor the one who serves me."

(2) In **Philippians 2:5-8** - "Your attitude should be the same as that of Christ Jesus: Who, being in very nature God, did not consider equality with God something to be grasped, but made himself nothing, taking the very nature of a

servant, being made in human likeness. And being found in appearance as a man, he humbled himself and became obedient to death- even death on a cross!"

(3) In **Matthew 6:33** - " But seek first his kingdom and his righteousness, and all these things will be given to you as well."

(4) In **John 15:4-5** - "Remain in me, and I will remain in you. No branch can bear fruit by itself; it must remain in the vine. Neither can you bear fruit unless you remain in me. "I am the vine; you are the branches. If a man remains in me and I in him, he will bear much fruit; apart from me you can do nothing."

(5) In **Matthew 4:19** - "Come, follow me," Jesus said, "and I will make you fishers of men."

(6) In **John 14:2-3** - " In my Father's house are many rooms; if it were not so, I would have told you. I am going there to prepare a place for you. And if I go and prepare a place for you, I will come back and take you to be with me that you also may be where I am."

(7) In **John 21 15-18** - " When they had finished eating, Jesus said to Simon Peter, "Simon son of John, do you truly love me more than these? "Yes, Lord," he said, "You know that I love you." Jesus said, "Feed my lambs. Again Jesus said, "Simon son of John, do you truly love me?" He answered, "Yes, Lord, you know that I love you." Jesus said, "Take care of my sheep. "The third time he said to him, "Simon son of John, do you love me?" Peter was hurt because Jesus asked him the third time, "Do you love me?" He said, "Lord, you know all things; you know that I love you. "Jesus said, "Feed my sheep. I tell you the truth, when you were younger you dressed yourself and went where you wanted; but when you are old you will stretch out your

hands, and someone else will dress you and lead you where you do not want to go."

(8) In **Matthew 22: 37-38** - " Jesus replied: " 'Love the Lord your God with all your heart and with all your soul and with all your mind. This is the first and greatest commandment."

(9) In **James 1:27** - "Religion that God our Father accepts as pure and faultless is this: to look after orphans and widows in their distress and to keep oneself from being polluted by the world. "

(10) In **Philippians 3:13-14** - "Brothers, I do not consider myself yet to have taken hold of it. But one thing I do: Forgetting what is behind and straining toward what is ahead, I press on toward the goal to win the prize for which God has called me heavenward in Christ Jesus."

(11) In **Romans 12:12** – "Be joyful in hope, patient in affliction, faithful in prayer."

(12) In **John 13:12-17** – "When he had finished washing their feet, he put on his clothes and returned to his place. "Do you understand what I have done for you?" he asked them. "You call me 'Teacher' and 'Lord,' and rightly so, for that is what I am. Now that I, your Lord and Teacher, have washed your feet, you also should wash one another's feet. I have set you an example that you should do as I have done for you. I tell you the truth, no servant is greater than his master, nor is a messenger greater than the one who sent him. Now that you know these things, you will be blessed if you do them."

(13) In **Luke 5:27-28** – "After this, Jesus went out and saw a tax collector by the name of Levi sitting at his tax booth. "Follow me," Jesus said to him, and Levi got up, left everything and followed him."

(14) In **Luke 9:23** - "Then he said to them all: 'If anyone would come after me, he must deny himself and take up his cross daily and follow me.'

(15) In **Matthew 12:30** - "He who is not with me is against me, and He who does not gather with me scatters."

So in the end, saying yes without hesitation to the Jesus' call to follow me requires the complete elimination of any and all excuses in our life. It requires a resolve on our part to be all that the Father has called us to be. To place the needs of others top of mind, front and center, It requires that we surrender and serve, It requires that we get focused with a singleness of purpose to align our will with His.

With this accomplished we can position our life to take advantage of His promises.

**Here are Eight (8) tips to Following In Life:**

1. **PUT GOD FIRST-** Christ must be at the center of everything. The Bible teaches us that our one and only priority is to keep Him, His Kingdom, and His righteousness first in everything. His will and our service to Him is our priority.

2. **Surrender-** His will be done!

3. **Serve-** Service is our calling;

4. **Take Responsibility -** You control your choices and are responsible for everything that happens and everything that you commit to.

5. **Limit Multi- tasking-** Performing several tasks less efficiently only serves to create anxiety, stress, and a sense of being out of control.

6. **Turn Off and Tune Out** – It is simply not possible or practical to believe that you can be "on" all 24/7/365. As the old saying reminds us if you attempt to burn the candle from both ends you will either get burned or if successful run out of light twice as fast.

7. **Eliminate the Clutter-** Don't allow your life or your day to be or get too full.

8. **Plan-** Set clear priorities for each area of your life. Remember to always make the decision to choose the activities that will assure you the greatest health, happiness and financial success in the long term.

**Six (6) Questions to answer Jesus' call to Follow Me:**

1. In the priorities of our life, where does God stand? Does He come before or after job, career, family, habits, or recreation?

2. Do I look out for myself, or am I concerned for the needs of others?

3. Do I care for the obligations and responsibilities that are mine as husband, father, friend, employee, employer, brother, sister, neighbor? Am I loyal and morally productive?

4. Do I seek God's will? Do I seek the things of God? Am I righteous and spiritual?

5. Am I obedient to His will and promptings?

6. Do I seek to faithfully follow His way, word, walk, and life?

**Consider these Five (5) Pitfalls to Following Jesus.**

**Five (5) Pitfalls to Follow Me to avoid:**

1) **Winning at all cost** – Your actions will tell the story as to whether or not things of this world or serving God is most important to you and your legacy.

2) **Political correctness-** You know both God's call to follow and His promise to each of us. Yet the marketplace of ideas hasn't taken the time to reflect on the cost of disobedience. Have you?

3) **Victimization, the 100-mile rule** – Life's hectic and you are not getting the attention you desire no one will ever know…except you!

4) **Lifestyles, Keeping up with the Jones** – You can't afford to both help a family in need and pop for drinks after work with the boss again this week. What do you decide to spend God's treasure on?

5) **Living by Default** – Are you humble or do you flaunt to impress. What you decide will speak volumes about where the treasure of your heart is.

Following His knowingly, willingly, and loving giving His blood at Calvary for us and His resurrection Jesus appeared again to His disciples at the Sea of Tiberias (Sea of Galilee). Let me set up the story for you.

Simon Peter, Thomas (nicknamed "Twin"), Nathanael from Cana in Galilee, the brothers James and John, and a couple of other disciples were together. Simon Peter, remember him from the beginning of Jesus' ministry announced, "I'm going fishing." Essentially saying Jesus has been crucified, I am lost therefore I am heading back to what I know best. I am going back to the fishing business. The Family business. The rest of them agreed, "We're going with you."

Think about it these were disciples who had walked with the Father for three years. Had watched Him perform miracle after miracle. Had listened to his words. Had been called not His servants but His friends. Lost, confused, leaderless, rudderless they could think of nothing to do except escape back to the future. Back to what they were comfortable with, what was safe.

They went out and got in the boat. They caught nothing that night. When the sun came up, Jesus was standing on the beach, but they didn't recognize him. Jesus spoke to them: "Good morning! Did you catch anything for breakfast?" They answered, "No." He said, "Throw the net off the right side of the boat and see what happens." They did what he said. All of a sudden there were so many fish in it, they weren't strong enough to pull it in. When Peter realized that it was the Master, he threw on some clothes and dove into the sea rushing off to greet Jesus.

After breakfast, Jesus said to Simon Peter, "Simon, son of John, do you love me more than these?" "Yes, Master, you know I love you." Jesus said, "Feed my lambs."

He then asked a second time, "Simon, son of John, do you love me?"

"Yes, Master, you know I love you." Jesus said, "Shepherd my sheep." Then he said it a third time: "Simon, son of John, do you love me?" Peter was upset that he asked for the third time, "Do you love me?" so he answered, "Master, you know everything there is to know. You've got to know that I love you."

Jesus said, "Feed my sheep. I'm telling you the very truth now:

When you were young you dressed yourself and went wherever you wished, but when you get old you'll have to stretch out your hands while someone else dresses you and takes you where you don't want to go." He said this to hint at the kind of death by which Peter would glorify God. And then he commanded, "Follow me."

As a final thought on this subject, do you believe that it was an accident, a mistake, a coincidence, or just luck that Jesus started and ended His walk and His ministry instructing us to follow? Do you think that Jesus was confused when He instructed us to feed His lambs, take care of His sheep, and to feed His sheep. In case you're confused His lambs and sheep are His people. He instructed us to take care, serve, and love His people.

Following Jesus' example I want to end up where I started. In the beginning I suggested that this is the most important decision that you will ever make in your entire life. Not just the most important decision for you personally but truly the most important decision that you will ever make in the lives of those you love. Take some time, consider the facts, and make a decision that will truly make a difference in both your life and in the lives of those who cross your path.

**PRACTICE:** To practice Jesus' call to follow pick three people you love and for one day each truly serve their needs. Then volunteer one day a week to help the disadvantaged. In your Success Journal write down how you made others feel and how that made you feel.

**PRAYER:** Heavenly Father all honor, praise and glory to you. Thank you for the many blessings that you have chosen to provide in my life. Father thank you for the honor of following you. I pray for the energy to seek your will, the discernment to know your will when you reveal it to me, and the obedience to immediately take action on that prompting. Thank you Father for being my rock. I love you Lord.

*On the other hand the likely hood of success increases greatly when we choose to commit and focus on the fact that our number one top priority is our relationship with the Father. This increase in likely hood of success is a direct result that our foundation to something other than selfishness in our process is so very much stronger.*

# CHAPTER SEVENTEEN

## CONCLUDING COMMENTS

Thankfully your success is not contingent upon any of these thoughts and truths being original to me. The words, thoughts, principles, doctrine, concepts and truths outlined in this book are not new. Christians with considerably more wisdom, discernment, and whose walk with the Lord is far more advanced than mine have spent a lifetime addressing these issues. I haven't been isolated away in some biblical scholar think tank putting this together. Instead I have been in prayer and in the word growing up in both body and spirit, blessed by both God and people.

Decision Time was carefully designed to come alongside you in your journey toward Christ likeness. Each of the eighteen chapters has attempted to address a key area of personal development and growth, using sound, biblical teaching and application.

Having made the decision to invest your financial, intellectual, and time resources in Decision Time, I hope that you have experienced an acceptable rate of return on your investment. Hopefully one take away is that you have become better equipped to evaluate your life and to grow intellectually, physically, spiritually, and socially, just as Jesus did while on earth.

It is my desire that the Father would use this book to help you achieve a life of health, balance, fulfillment and success. It is my sincere prayer that Decision Time has served to motivate you to grow in every area of life, to seek balance and a godly perspective, and to pursue Christ with every thought and action.

Let us join together today deciding not to follow the same tired and rocky road that we often find ourselves traveling over and over again making the same old mistakes and poor judgments. In its place, let's journey together on the Real Path to explore and experience the way Jesus lived on earth.

His example can be summarized in one simple sentence: "Jesus grew in wisdom and stature, and in favor with God and men" **(Luke 2:52 NIV)**.

**In Luke 2:41-52** we are reminded that every year Jesus' parents traveled to Jerusalem for the Feast of Passover. When he was twelve years old, they went up as they always did for the Feast. When it was over and they left for home, the child Jesus stayed behind in Jerusalem, but his parents didn't know it. Thinking he was somewhere in the company of pilgrims, they journeyed for a whole day and then began looking for him among relatives and neighbors. When they didn't find him, they went back to Jerusalem looking for him.

The next day they found him in the Temple seated among the teachers, listening to them and asking questions. The teachers were all quite taken with him, impressed with the sharpness of his answers. But his parents were not impressed; they were upset and hurt.

His mother said, "Young man, why have you done this to us? Your father and I have been half out of our minds looking for you."

He said, "Why were you looking for me? Didn't you know that I had to be here, dealing with the things of my Father?" But they had no idea what he was talking about.

So he went back to Nazareth with them, and lived obediently with them. His mother held these things dearly, deep within herself. And **Jesus matured, growing up in both body and spirit, blessed by both God and people.**

If you are like me, you value the Father's teaching and example greatly as you look to fulfill the promise for our lives that the Father has prepared for us.

Through his teaching he challenges each of us to continue to mature, growing up in both body and spirit, blessed by both God and other Christians. Remember that in **Proverbs 27:17** we are taught "As iron sharpens iron, so one man sharpens another."

He said it, he lived it, he meant it, and as a Christian I believe it. As such this challenge resonates greatly with me. Based on Jesus' example it is clear that one cannot fully develop spiritually unless one develops in life's other areas as well. Those areas include intellectual, physical, social, and emotional aspects of our lives.

You cannot neglect one of these areas without endangering your growth in all of them. Likewise, you cannot grow in any one of these areas without also having an effect on all the others. In **Proverbs 11:1** we are instructed that "A false balance is abomination to the Lord: but a just weight is his delight."

To that end, consider allowing Decision Time to come alongside you in your journey to develop a Christ like maturity. Hopefully, you will find that each chapter addresses a key area of growth, using a method of sound, biblical teaching and application that works both in the short-term and long-term.

My prayer is that you will read and apply every word of this resource, choosing to pursue personal Christian maturity wholeheartedly. When you do, an incredible journey awaits as you grow in much the same way as Jesus did. Frankly, I'm excited about the opportunity to join you on this journey of learning and growing in Christ together.

What we have accomplished is to take 2000 years of scripture, doctrine, example, experience, and truth all of which is time tested, proven and positioned it in such a way that it flows effectively and is easy to get our minds around. The awesome news is that the word is the same today as yesterday and will be the same tomorrow. The Father offers us one consistent road to success to follow. There are no detours or side roads just one perfectly paved highway.

Forty-Eight thousand (48,000) words or so and if I were a truly effective communicator I could have made the case in just four (4) words.

The Four (4) words to which I am referring were taught to us by Jesus and can be found beginning in Matthew 6:9. Jesus taught and instructed that. This, then, is how you should pray". The four (4) words found in the Lords Prayer are "Your Will Be Done". That doesn't mean your will or my will; it literally means the Father's will be done.

At this point more than likely this doesn't need to be pointed out but it is extremely fortunate for all of us that we do not have to rely on my ability or book to figure all this out. The Father wrote the thesis that figures this all out. It is called the Bible, perhaps you have heard of it. What we know is that by definition God cannot lie and he tells us that every word that He speaks is flawless so our blue print is His inspired word.

**Here is what the Lord says about word and beliefs:**

1) **In 2 Samuel 22:31** "As for God, his way is perfect; the word of the LORD is flawless. He is a shield for all who take refuge in him

2) **In Job 11:4** You say to God, 'my beliefs are flawless and I am pure in your sight.

3) **In Psalm 12:6** And the words of the LORD are flawless, like silver refined in a furnace of clay, purified seven times.

4) **In Psalm 18:30** As for God, his way is perfect; the word of the LORD is flawless. He is a shield for all who take refuge in him.

5) **In Proverbs 30:5** "Every word of God is flawless; he is a shield to those who take refuge in him

This then becomes the point at which we take the opportunity to circle back around to tie this all together.

First, I hope that I have satisfactorily made the case as to why all these different disciplines were necessary to address in a book about Christ-centered values and decision-making? To restate based on Jesus' example, it is clear that one cannot fully develop spiritually unless one develops in life's other areas as well.

Second, having read, completed, considered, and begun to change the process you utilize for Christ-centered decision-making, can we agree that just making the decision to change in no way, guarantees that a change will ensue. If all it took to enact change was to make the decision to change, we would all be perfect. As I have said to my children for years if it were easy anyone could do it. The problem then would be that it would drastically reduce the value of what we were accomplishing. In the same light, if a mere decision to change actually insured change, all of our New Year's resolutions would immediately and successfully remain a permanent part of our lives. Each of us having lived through a few rounds of New Year's Eve resolutions are all well aware of the fallacy of that theory.

Third, there is no question or quarrel that a good decision can be a catalyst for change. But it is also fairly obvious that without the structured discipline of an effective process with an under girding of Christian values, long-term successful change would be more a matter of luck than that of a plan. In which case long-term success is dubious.

Fourth, the reality is that if we want to guarantee that a change will actually occur, we have to initiate and implement a well thought out, plan, and Christ-centered process. A Godly process that requires us to surrender our own will, needs, and desires and replaces them with the best interests of others.

Fifth, in order to increase the likelihood that your decision making will successfully endure the test of time you need look no further than the way, walk, will, and word of the Father for your example.

Sixth, it is important that you allow yourself the opportunity to develop a complete skill set to effectively initiate and implement a consistent long-term strategic success plan. Toward this end, you need to consider praying and being in the word daily. Hopefully, we have helped equip you with a wide variety of skills that will be needed to build a truly successful Christ-centered life and decision process. To this end, I would encourage you to memorize the scripture found in this book. In fact, consider listing out the scripture in one column. In the center column rewrite the scripture in your own words. In a third column indicate how the scripture will make a difference in your lifestyle and decision making process. Then commit to showing and speaking with an accountability partner about your process.

Seventh, these skills interact with each other for true success. We are taught in **1 Corinthians 12:11-13** - "All these are the work of one and the same Spirit, and he gives them to each one, just as he determines. The body is a unit, though it is made up of many parts; and though all its parts are many, they form one body. So it is with Christ. For we were all baptized by one Spirit into one body—whether Jews or Greeks, slave or free—and we were all given the one Spirit to drink."

In the same way that the body is made up of many moving parts all connected as one unit, it is also true that effective, successful, and cohesive decisions result from all of these afore mentioned skills working in unison as one. In this way, we form a basis for success, happiness, peace, and eternal love.

Eighth, after reading this you may be questioning why so much scripture has been included. Not withstanding the fact that I am a Christian, this book is written for one reason and one reason only, that being to provide you with a guide for Christian living that will equip you for a lifetime of successful decision-making. Decision- making which will positively serve all those who cross your path.

The word is clear that without your complete surrender to the will of the Father your chances of long term success and happiness with regard to your decision process is questionable at best. The likely hood of success increases greatly when we choose to commit and focus on the fact that our number one top priority is our relationship with the Father.

A direct result of trading self-centeredness for Christ-centeredness is a foundation and process that is very much stronger and has staying power. To that end, I think that we can all find agreement in the fact that you can't know the Father without knowing his walk, way, word, and you can't know his way, walk, and word without knowing scripture. Most importantly you can't walk with the Father until you align your will with His which requires surrender and a Christ-centered lifestyle. Lessons taught to us in scripture.

Ninth, where does Christ-centeredness come into play and how does it relate to my ability to render effective decisions? For leaders, the process of finding and owning their Christ-centeredness involves the decision and ability to move away from any and all victimization, self centeredness, me first attitude, what's in it for me belief system, and the I am in control thought processes. Real leaders stake claim to their Christ Likeness when they demonstrate that they are strong enough to surrender control, serve others, seek the Father's will, witness, testify, and love their neighbor without judging.

Finding your Christ-centered life involves gaining leadership through humility and getting stronger as a direct result of a willingness to invest emotionally in God's people and His Kingdom.

After reading Decision Time, working through the questions section, and applying the practice principles I assume that you will be well on your way to developing the Christian lifestyle that you seek and which will serve you well. I applaud your journey and hope that I can play an active role in your growth and success. To that end, please know that I would love to hear from each of you with questions, concerns, differences of opinions and approaches. Please consider following up with me.

His will be done!

Contact me on the web at realpathcoaching.com: e-mail me at rplcoaching@gmail.com, www.realpathcoachinginstitute.com or better yet call me at 843 589-9236

*Philippians 3:13-14 - "Brothers, I do not consider myself yet to have taken hold of it. But one thing I do: Forgetting what is behind and straining toward what is ahead, I press on toward the goal to win the prize for which God has called me heavenward in Christ Jesus."*

# CHAPTER EIGHTEEN

## SCRIPTURE GLOSSARY
## THE OLD TESTAMENT

**Genesis 1:1- 2:4** we are instructed that God created Heaven and Earth. We are told that First God created the Heavens and Earth. That literally means all that we see and all that we don't see was created by the heavenly father. The picture is communicated that Earth was a soup of nothingness, a bottomless emptiness, and an inky blackness. God's Spirit brooded like a bird above the watery abyss. God spoke: "Light!" And light appeared. God saw that light was good and separated light from dark. God named the light Day and he named the dark Night. It was evening and then it was morning. On Day One God spoke: "Sky! In the middle of the waters; he separated water from water!" God made the sky. He separated the water under sky from the water above sky. And there it was: he named sky the Heavens. It was evening and then it was morning. On Day Two God spoke: "Separate! Water-beneath-Heaven, gather into one place; Land, appear!" And there it was. God named the land Earth. He named the pooled water Ocean. God saw that it was good. God spoke: "Earth, green up! Grow all varieties of seed-bearing plants, every sort

149

of fruit-bearing tree." And there it was. Earth produced green seed-bearing plants, all varieties, and fruit-bearing trees of all sorts God saw that it was good. It was evening and then it was morning. On Day Three God spoke: "Lights! Come out! Shine in Heaven's sky! Separate Day from Night. Marking seasons and days and years, Lights in Heaven's sky to give light to Earth." And there it was. God made two big lights, the larger to take charge of Day, The smaller to be in charge of Night; and he made the stars. God placed them in the heavenly sky to light up Earth And oversee Day and Night, to separate light and dark. God saw that it was good. It was evening and then it was morning. On Day Four God spoke: "Swarm, Ocean, with fish and all sea life! Birds, fly through the sky over Earth!" God created the huge whales, all the swarm of life in the waters, and every kind and species of flying birds. God saw that it was good. God blessed them: "Prosper! Reproduce! Fill Ocean! Birds reproduce on Earth!" It was evening and then it was morning. On Day Five God spoke: "Earth, generate life! Every sort and kind: Cattle and reptiles and wild animals of all varieties." And there it was: Wild animals of every species, Cattle of all kinds, every sort of reptile and bug. God saw that it was good. God spoke: "Let us make human beings in our image, make them reflecting our nature So they can be responsible for the fish in the sea, the birds in the air, the cattle, And, yes, Earth itself, and every animal that moves on the face of Earth." God created human beings; he created them God -like, Reflecting God's nature. He created them male and female. God blessed them: "Prosper! Reproduce! Fill Earth! Take charge! Be responsible for fish in the sea and birds in the air, for every living thing that moves on the face of Earth." Then God said, "I've given you every sort of seed-bearing plant on Earth and every kind of fruit-bearing tree, given them to you for food. To all animals and all birds, everything that moves and breathes, I give whatever grows out of the ground for food." And there it was. God looked over everything he had made; it was so good, so very good! It was evening and then it was morning. On Day Six Heaven and Earth were finished, down to the last detail. By the seventh day God had finished his work. On the seventh day he rested from all his work. God blessed the seventh day. He made it a Holy Day because on that day he rested from his work, the entire creating God had done. This is the story of how it all started, of Heaven and Earth and when they were created.

**Genesis 2:23- 24** "This is now bone of my bones and flesh of my flesh; she shall be called 'woman, 'for she was taken out of man. "For this reason a man will leave his father and mother and be united to his wife, and they will become one flesh.

**Genesis 3:1-7** Now the serpent was more crafty than any of the wild animals the LORD God had made. He said to the woman, "Did God really say, 'You must not eat from any tree in the garden'?" The woman said to the serpent, "We may eat fruit from the trees in the garden, but God did say, 'you must not eat fruit from the tree that is in the middle of the garden, and you must not touch it, or you will die.' " "You will not surely die," the serpent said to the woman." For God knows that when you eat of it your eyes will be opened, and you will be like God, knowing good and evil." When the woman saw that the fruit of the tree was good for food and pleasing to the eye, and also desirable for gaining wisdom, she took some and ate it. She also gave some to her husband, who was with her, and he ate it. Then the eyes of both of them were opened, and they realized they were naked; so they sewed fig leaves together and made coverings for themselves.

**Genesis 5:2** "He created them male and female and blessed them."

**Genesis 15:1** - "Do not be afraid, Abram. I am your shield, your very great reward."-Fear

**Genesis 24:67** - Isaac brought her into the tent of his mother Sarah, and he married Rebekah. So she became his wife, and he loved her; and Isaac was comforted after his mother's death. - Intro

**Genesis 29:10-11** -When Jacob saw Rachel daughter of Laban, his mother's brother, and Laban's sheep, he went over and rolled the stone away from the mouth of the well and watered his uncle's sheep. Then Jacob kissed Rachel and began to weep aloud. - Intro

**Genesis 29:18-20** -Jacob was in love with Rachel and said, "I'll work for you seven years in return for your younger daughter Rachel." Laban said, "It's better that I give her to you than to some other man. Stay here with me." So Jacob served seven years to get Rachel, but they seemed like only a few days to him because of his love for her. - Intro

**Exodus 33:16** – Then Moses said to Him " If your Presence does not go with us, do not bring us up from here."-Success

**Deuteronomy 6:6-9** - "These commandments that I give you today are to be upon your hearts. Impress them on your children. Talk about them when you sit at home and when you walk along the road, when you lie down and when you get up. Tie them as symbols on your hands and bind them on your foreheads.  Write them on the doorframes of your houses and on your gates." - Fatherhood

**Deuteronomy 18:15-** Mosses wrote "The Lord your God will raise up for you a prophet like me from among you—from your fellow Israelites; you must listen to him." – Listening

**Joshua 1:9** - "Have I not commanded you? Be strong and courageous. Do not be terrified; do not be discouraged, for the LORD your God will be with you wherever you go."- Fear

**Judges 7:3** – "announce now to the people, 'Anyone who trembles with fear may turn back and leave Mount Gilead.' " So twenty-two thousand men left, while ten thousand remained."-Fear

**1SAMUEL 8:7** - " And the LORD told him: "Listen to all that the people are saying to you; it is not you they have rejected, but they have rejected me as their king." – Leadership

**1 Samuel 3:9-** "So Eli told Samuel, "Go and lie down, and if he calls you, say, 'Speak, LORD, for your servant is listening.' " So Samuel went and lay down in his place."

**1 Samuel 3:10-** "The LORD came and stood there, calling as at the other times, "Samuel! Samuel!" Then Samuel said, "Speak, for your servant is listening."- Listening

**1 Samuel 16:7** - But the Lord said to Samuel, "Do not consider his appearance or his height, for I have rejected him. The Lord does not look at the things man looks at. Man looks at the outward appearance, but the Lord looks at the heart. – Intro

**2 Samuel 22:31** - "As for God, his way is perfect; the word of the LORD is flawless. He is a shield for all who take refuge in him. - conclusion

**Job 11:4** - you say to God, 'my beliefs are flawless and I am pure in your sight. - Conclusion

**Job 31:6 -** "Let me be weighed in an even balance, that God may know mine integrity." -Balance

**Psalms 1:1-2 -** "Blessed is the man who does not walk in the counsel of the wicked or stand in the way of sinners or sit in the seat of mockers. But his delight is in the law of the LORD, and on his law he meditates day and night." – Prioritizing

**Psalm 12:6-** And the words of the LORD are flawless, like silver refined in a furnace of clay, purified seven times. - Conclusion

Psalm 14:1 –"The fool says in his heart, "There is no God." They are corrupt, their deeds are vile; there is no one who does good."-Success

**Psalm 15:2-5** -He whose walk is blameless and who does what is righteous, who speaks the truth from his heart And has no slander on tongue, who does his neighbor no wrong and casts no slur on his fellow man, Who despises a vile man but honors those who fear the Lord, who keeps his oath even when it hurts, Who lends his money without usury and does not accept a bribe against the innocent. He who does these things will never be shaken. – Intro

**Psalm 18:30** - As for God, his way is perfect; the word of the LORD is flawless. He is a shield for all who take refuge in him. - Conclusion

**Psalm 23:4 -** "Even though I walk through the valley of the shadow of death, I will fear no evil, for you are with me; your rod and your staff, they comfort me." –Fear

**Psalm 103:13 -** "As a father has compassion on his children, so the LORD has compassion on those who fear him" – Fatherhood, Intro

**Psalms 119:11** - " I have hidden your word in my heart that I might not sin against you."- Balance

**Psalm 128:1-4** - Blessed are all who fear the Lord, who walk in his ways. You will eat the fruit of your labor; blessings and prosperity will be yours. Your wife will be like a fruitful vine within your house; your sons will be like olive shoots around your table. Thus is the man blessed who fears the Lord. -Intro

**Proverbs 3:13-18 -** Blessed is the man who finds wisdom, the man who gains understanding, for she is more profitable than silver and yields better returns than gold. She is more precious than rubies; nothing you desire can compare with her. Long life is in her right hand; in her left hand are riches and honor. Her ways are pleasant ways, and all her paths are peace. She is a tree of life to those who embrace her; those who lay hold of her will be blessed. - Intro

**Proverbs 6:20-22-** My son, keep your father's commands and do not forsake your mother's teaching. Bind them upon your heart forever; fasten them around your neck. When you walk, they will guide you; when you sleep, they will speak to you. - Intro

**Proverbs 7:1-5 -** My son, keep my words and store up my commands within you. Keep my commands and you will live; guard my teachings as the apple of your eye. Bind them on your fingers; write them on the tablet of your heart. Say to wisdom, "You are my sister," and call understanding your kinsman; they will keep you from the adulteress, from the wayward wife with her seductive words. -Intro

**Proverbs 8:17 -** " I love those who love me, and those who seek me find me."-Balance

**Proverbs 10:9 -** The man of integrity walks securely, but he who takes crooked paths will be found out. - Intro

**Proverbs 11:1 -** "A false balance is abomination to the Lord: but a just weight is his delight." –Balance

**Proverbs 11:27-** "For one, he says you'll be respected if you set good goals."- Goals

**Proverbs 13:16-**"A wise man thinks ahead, a fool doesn't and even brags about it."-Goals

**Proverbs 16:9 -** "We should make plans, counting on God to direct us."-Goals

**Proverbs 17:27** - A man of knowledge uses words with restraint, and a man of understanding is even-tempered. - Intro

**Proverbs 18:2-** Solomon offers a direct open evaluation of those who would rather talk than listen: "A fool finds no pleasure in understanding but delights in airing his own opinions". - Listening

**Proverbs 18:13-** it is written, "Spouting off before listening to the facts is both shameful and foolish." – Listening

**Proverbs 18:16** - "A man's gift makes room for him, and brings him before great men."- Talents

**Proverbs 19:13** - " A foolish son is his father's ruin, and a quarrelsome wife is like a constant dripping." - Fatherhood

**Proverbs 20:6-** Many a man claims to have unfailing love, but a faithful man who can find? - Intro

**Proverbs 20:7** - "The righteous man leads a blameless life; blessed are his children after him." – Fatherhood, Intro

**Proverbs 22:6** - "Train a child in the way he should go, and when he is old he will not turn from It." - Fatherhood

**Proverbs 24:3-**"Any enterprise is built by wise planning, becomes strong through common sense, and profits wonderfully by keeping abreast of the facts."-Goals

**Proverbs 27:17** – "As iron sharpens iron, so one man sharpens another."-Success

**Proverbs 28:6** - Better a poor man whose walk is blameless than a rich man whose ways are perverse. - Intro

**Proverbs 29:23 -** A man's pride brings him low, but a man of lowly spirit gains honor. – Intro

**Proverbs 30:5-** "Every word of God is flawless; he is a shield to those who take refuge in him. - Conclusion

**1 Chronicles 28:9 -** And you, my son Solomon, acknowledge the God of your father, and serve him with wholehearted devotion and with a willing mind, for the Lord searches every heart and understands every motive behind the thoughts. If you seek him, he will be found by you; but if you forsake him, he will reject you forever. Intro

**Ecclesiastes 3:8 –** "A time to love, and a time to hate; a time for war, and a time for peace."-Time

**Isaiah 40:31-** "but those who trust in the Lord will find new strength. They will soar high on wings like Eagles. They will run and not grow weary. They will walk and not faint." -Looking Forward

**Isaiah 41:10 -** "So do not fear, for I am with you; do not be dismayed, for I am your God. I will strengthen you and help you; I will uphold you with my righteous right hand."-Fear

**Isaiah 55:8-9 -** "For my thoughts are not your thoughts neither are your ways my ways," declares the LORD. "As the heavens are higher than the earth, so are my ways higher than your ways and my thoughts than your thoughts. –Success

**ISAIAH 58:7 -** "Is it not to share your food with the hungry and to provide the poor wanderer with shelter—when you see the naked, to clothe him and not to turn away from your own flesh and blood?" - Leadership

**Jeremiah 17:9-10 -** "The heart is deceitful above all things and beyond cure. Who can understand it? "I the LORD search the heart and examine the mind, to reward a man according to his conduct, according to what his deeds deserve."-Success

**Daniel 1:8** - But Daniel resolved not to defile himself - Intro

**DANIEL 2:30** - "As for me, this mystery has been revealed to me, not because I have greater wisdom than other living men, but so that you, O king, may know the interpretation and that you may understand what went through your mind." – Leadership

**Malachi 4:6** - "He will turn the hearts of the fathers to their children, and the hearts of the children to their fathers; or else I will come and strike the land with a curse." – Fatherhood, Intro

# THE NEW TESTAMENT

**Matthew 4:19** - "Come, follow me," Jesus said, "and I will make you fishers of men."- Follow

**Matthew 5:6** - "Blessed are those who hunger and thirst for righteousness, for they will be filled."- Balance, Prioritizing

**Matthew 6:19** - "Do not store up for yourselves treasures on earth, where moth and rust destroy, and where thieves break in and steal." - Prioritizing

**Matthew 6:31-33** -"So do not worry, saying, 'What shall we eat?' or 'What shall we drink?' or 'What shall we wear? 'For the pagans run after all these things, and your heavenly Father knows that you need them. But seek first his kingdom and his righteousness, and all these things will be given to you as well." - Prioritizing

**Matthew 6:33** – "but seek first the kingdom of God and his righteousness, and all these things will be added to you."- Time, Balance, Revolution, Follow

**Matthew 7:7-11** - "Ask and it will be given to you; seek and you will find; knock and the door will be opened to you. For everyone who asks receives; he who seeks finds; and to him who knocks, the door will be opened."- Revolution

**Matthew 7:12** -- In everything, do to others what you would have them do to you - Intro

**Matthew 11:27-29** -"All things have been committed to me by my Father. No one knows the Son except the Father, and no one knows the Father except the Son and those to whom the Son chooses to reveal him. Come to me, all you who are weary and burdened, and I will give you rest. Take my yoke upon you and learn from me, for I am gentle and humble in heart, and you will find rest for your souls." – Leadership

**Matthew 12:30** - "He who is not with me is against me, and He who does not gather with me scatters." Follow

**Matthew 16:8-10** - Aware of their discussion, Jesus asked, "You of little faith, why are you talking among yourselves about having no bread? Do you still not understand? Don't you remember the five loaves for the five thousand, and how many basketfuls you gathered? Or the seven loaves for the four thousand, and how many basketfuls you gathered? - Signs

**Matthew 16: 24-26** - "Then said Jesus unto his disciples, If any man will come after me, let him deny himself, and take up his cross, and follow me. For whosoever will save his life shall lose it: and whosoever will lose his life for my sake shall find it. For what is a man profited, if he shall gain the whole world, and lose his own soul? Or what shall a man give in exchange for his soul?" Balance

**Matthew 18: 1-4**- " At that time the disciples came to Jesus and asked, "Who is the greatest in the kingdom of heaven?" He called a little child and had him stand among them. And he said: "I tell you the truth, unless you change and become like little children, you will never enter the kingdom of heaven. Therefore, whoever humbles himself like this child is the greatest in the kingdom of heaven." – Leadership

**Matthew 18:6** - "But if anyone causes one of these little ones who believe in me to sin, it would be better for him to have a large millstone hung around his neck and to be drowned in the depths of the sea." – Fatherhood

**MATTHEW 20:25-28** - "Jesus called them together and said, "You know that the rulers of the Gentiles lord it over them, and their high officials exercise authority over them. Not so with you. Instead, whoever wants to become great among you must be your servant, and whoever wants to be first must be your slave— just as the Son of Man did not come to be served, but to serve, and to give his life as a ransom for many." – Leadership

**Matthew 22: 37-38** - " Jesus replied: " 'Love the Lord your God with all your heart and with all your soul and with all your mind. This is the first and greatest commandment." –Balance, Follow

**Matthew 26:41** - Watch and pray so that you will not fall into temptation. The spirit is willing, but the body is weak. - Intro

**Mark 4:19** -" but the worries of this life, the deceitfulness of wealth and the desires for other things come in and choke the word, making it unfruitful." – Success, Follow

**Mark 4:20** -" Others, like seed sown on good soil, hear the word, accept it, and produce a crop—thirty, sixty or even a hundred times what was sown." – Success

**Mark 6:45-52** - Immediately Jesus made his disciples get into the boat and go on ahead of him to Bethsaida, while he dismissed the crowd. After leaving them, he went up on a mountainside to pray. When evening came, the boat was in the middle of the lake, and he was alone on land. He saw the disciples straining at the oars, because the wind was against them. About the fourth watch of the night he went out to them, walking on the lake. He was about to pass by them, but when they saw him walking on the lake, they thought he was a ghost. They cried out, because they all saw him and were terrified. Immediately he spoke to them and said, "Take courage! It is I. Don't be afraid." Then he climbed into the boat with them, and the wind died down. They were completely amazed, for they had not understood about the loaves; their hearts were hardened. - Signs

**Mark 9: 4** – " The Lord warned, "Whoever has ears to hear had better listen!" and again in verse 23 He said "If anyone has ears to hear, he had better listen!" - Listening

**Mark 10: 45** - "For even the Son of Man did not come to be served, but to serve, and to give His life as a ransom for many" – POF

**Mark 11:12-14** - The next day as they were leaving Bethany, Jesus was hungry. Seeing in the distance a fig tree in leaf, he went to find out if it had any fruit. When he reached it, he found nothing but leaves, because it was not the season for figs. Then he said to the tree, "May no one ever eat fruit from you again." And his disciples heard him say it. - Signs

**Mark 16:15** - "And he said to them, "Go into all the world and preach the gospel to all creation." – Revolution

**Luke 2:36-38** - "There was also a prophetess, Anna, the daughter of Phanuel, of the tribe of Asher. She was very old; she had lived with her husband seven years after her marriage, and then was a widow until she was eighty-four. She never left the temple but worshiped night and day, fasting and praying. Coming up to them at that very moment, she gave thanks to

God and spoke about the child to all who were looking forward to the redemption of Jerusalem." – FIP

**Luke 5:27-28** –"After this, Jesus went out and saw a tax collector by the name of Levi sitting at his tax booth. "Follow me," Jesus said to him, and Levi got up, left everything and followed him."- Follow

**Luke 6:31** - Do to others as you would have them do to you. – Intro

**Luke 9:12-17** - Late in the afternoon the Twelve came to him and said, "Send the crowd away so they can go to the surrounding villages and countryside and find food and lodging, because we are in a remote place here. "He replied, "You give them something to eat. "They answered, "We have only five loaves of bread and two fish—unless we go and buy food for all this crowd." (About five thousand men were there.) But he said to his disciples, "Have them sit down in groups of about fifty each." The disciples did so, and everybody sat down. Taking the five loaves and the two fish and looking up to heaven, he gave thanks and broke them. Then he gave them to the disciples to set before the people. They all ate and were satisfied, and the disciples picked up twelve basketfuls of broken pieces that were left over. - Signs

**Luke 9:23** - "Then he said to them all: 'If anyone would come after me, he must deny himself and take up his cross daily and follow me.'-Follow

**Luke 10:41-42** - "Martha, Martha," the Lord answered, "you are worried and upset about many things, but only one thing is needed. Mary has chosen what is better, and it will not be taken away from her." – Prioritizing

**Luke 11:27-28** - "As Jesus was saying these things, a woman in the crowd called out, "Blessed is the mother who gave you birth and nursed you." Jesus replied, "Blessed rather are those who hear the word of God and obey It." - Signs

**Luke 12:15** - "Then he said to them, "Watch out! Be on your guard against all kinds of greed; a man's life does not consist in the abundance of his possessions." – Balance, Prioritizing

**Luke 16:10** - Whoever can be trusted with very little can also be trusted with much, and whoever is dishonest with very little will also be dishonest with much. - Intro

**Luke 18:1** - "Then Jesus told his disciples a parable to show them that they should always pray and not give up. Therefore I remind you to stir up the gift of God which is in you through the laying on of my hands." FIP

**Luke 23:34** - Jesus said, "Father, forgive them, for they do not know what they are doing."- POF

**John 1:1** - "In the beginning was the Word, and the Word was with God, and the Word was God." – Prioritizing

**John 3:3** In reply Jesus answered, " I tell you the truth, no one can see the kingdom of God unless he is born again." Dedication

**John 4:15** - "Whoever confesses that Jesus is the Son of God, God abides in him, and he in God." 1 Thessalonians 5:4-5 – "But you, brothers, are not in darkness so that this day should surprise you like a thief. You are all sons of the light and sons of the day. We do not belong to the night or to the darkness." – Revolution

**John 6:16-21** - When evening came, his disciples went down to the lake, where they got into a boat and set off across the lake for Capernaum. By now it was dark, and Jesus had not yet joined them.  A strong wind was blowing and the waters grew rough. When they had rowed three or three and a half miles, they saw Jesus approaching the boat, walking on the water; and they were terrified. But he said to them, "It is I; don't be afraid." Then they were willing to take him into the boat, and immediately the boat reached the shore where they were heading. - Signs

**John 7:24** - Stop judging by mere appearances, and make a right judgment. - Intro

**JOHN 10:11**- "I am the good shepherd. The good shepherd lays down his life for the sheep" – Leadership

**John 12:9 -** Meanwhile a large crowd of Jews found out that Jesus was there and came, not only because of him but also to see Lazarus, whom he had raised from the dead. - Signs

**John 12:24-26 -** "I tell you the truth, unless a kernel of wheat falls to the ground and dies, it remains only a single seed. But if it dies, it produces many seeds. The man who loves his life will lose it, while the man who hates his life in this world will keep it for eternal life. Whoever serves me must follow me; and where I am, my servant also will be. My Father will honor the one who serves me."

**John 12:25** "The man who loves his life will lose it, while the man who hates his life in this world will keep it for eternal life." – Revolution

**JOHN 13:5** - "After that, he poured water into a basin and began to wash his disciples' feet, drying them with the towel that was wrapped around him." – Leadership

**John 12:24-26 -** "I tell you the truth, unless a kernel of wheat falls to the ground and dies, it remains only a single seed. But if it dies, it produces many seeds. The man who loves his life will lose it, while the man who hates his life in this world will keep it for eternal life. Whoever serves me must follow me;

and where I am, my servant also will be. My Father will honor the one who serves me." - Follow

**John 13:12-17** –"When he had finished washing their feet, he put on his clothes and returned to his place. "Do you understand what I have done for you?" he asked them. "You call me 'Teacher' and 'Lord,' and rightly so, for that is what I am. Now that I, your Lord and Teacher, have washed your feet, you also should wash one another's feet. I have set you an example that you should do as I have done for you. I tell you the truth, no servant is greater than his master, nor is a messenger greater than the one who sent him. Now that you know these things, you will be blessed if you do them."- Follow

**John 14:2-3 - "** In my Father's house are many rooms; if it were not so, I would have told you. I am going there to prepare a place for you. And if I go and prepare a place for you, I will come back and take you to be with me that you also may be where I am."-Follow

**John 14:6 – "** Jesus answered, "I am the way and the truth and the life. No one comes to the Father except through me."- Revolution

**John 14:26-27** - "But the Counselor, the Holy Spirit, whom the Father will send in my name, will teach you all things and will remind you of everything I have said to you. Peace I leave with you; my peace I give you. I do not give to you as the world gives. Do not let your hearts be troubled and do not be afraid."- Fear

**John 15:4-5** - "Remain in me, and I will remain in you. No branch can bear fruit by itself; it must remain in the vine. Neither can you bear fruit unless you remain in me. "I am the vine; you are the branches. If a man remains in me and I in him, he will bear much fruit; apart from me you can do nothing."-Follow

**John 20:30** - Jesus did many other miraculous signs in the presence of his disciples, which are not recorded in this book. - Signs

**John 21 15-18** - " I When they had finished eating, Jesus said to Simon Peter, "Simon son of John, do you truly love me more than these? "Yes, Lord," he said, "You know that I love you." Jesus said, "Feed my lambs. Again Jesus said, "Simon son of John, do you truly love me?" He answered, "Yes, Lord, you know that I love you." Jesus said, "Take care of my sheep. "The third time he said to him, "Simon son of John, do you love me?" Peter was hurt because Jesus asked him the third time, "Do you love me?" He said, "Lord, you know all things; you know that I love you. "Jesus said, "Feed my sheep. I tell you the truth, when you were younger you dressed yourself and went where you wanted; but when you are old you will stretch out your hands, and someone else will dress you and lead you where you do not want to go."- Follow

**1 John 4:18** - "There is no fear in love. But perfect love drives out fear, because fear has to do with punishment. The one who fears is not made perfect in love." – Fear

**Acts 4:30** - Stretch out your hand to heal and perform miraculous signs and wonders through the name of your holy servant Jesus."- Signs

**1 Corinthians 7:34** - But a married man is concerned about the affairs of this world—how he can please his wife— and his interests are divided. An unmarried woman or virgin is concerned about the Lord's affairs: Her aim is to be devoted to the Lord in both body and spirit. But a married woman is concerned about the affairs of this world—how she can please her husband. I am saying this for your own good, not to restrict you, but that you may live in a right way in undivided devotion to the Lord. Intro

**1 Corinthians 8:13** - Therefore, if what I eat causes my brother to fall into sin, I will never eat meat again, so that I will not cause him to fall. –POF

**1 Corinthians 9:20-22** To the Jews I became like a Jew, to win the Jews. To those under the law I became like one under the law (though I myself am not under the law), so as to win those under the law. To those not having the law I became like one not having the law (though I am not free from God's law but am under Christ's law), so as to win those not having the law. To the weak I became weak, to win the weak. I have become all things to all men so that by all possible means I might save some. -Dedication

**1 Corinthians 10:13** - No temptation has seized you except what is common to man. And God is faithful; he will not let you be tempted beyond what you can bear. But when you are tempted, he will also provide a way out so that you can stand up under it. - Intro

**1 Corinthians 10:24** - Nobody should seek his own good, but the good of others- POF.

**1 Corinthians 11:3** - "But I want you to know that the head of every man is Christ, the head of woman is man, and the head of Christ is God"- Intro

**1 Corinthians 11:8-9,11-12** - For man did not come from woman, but woman from man, neither was man created for woman, but woman for man. In the Lord, however, woman is not independent of man, nor is man independent of woman. For as woman came from man, so also man is born of woman. But everything comes from God. - Intro

**1 Corinthians 12:11-13** - "All these are the work of one and the same Spirit, and he gives them to each one, just as he determines. The body is a unit, though it is made up of many parts; and though all its parts are many, they form one body. So it is with Christ. For we were all baptized by one Spirit into one body—whether Jews or Greeks, slave or free—and we were all given the one Spirit to drink." – Concluding Comments

**2 Corinthians 5:10-11** - "For we must all appear before the judgment seat of Christ, that each one may receive what is due him for the things done while in the body, whether good or bad. Since, then, we know what it is to fear the Lord, we try to persuade men. What we are is plain to God, and I hope it is also plain to your conscience."- Fear

**Hebrews 7:26-28** we are instructed that Such a high priest meets our need one who is holy, blameless, pure, set apart from sinners, exalted above the heavens. Unlike the other high priests, he does not need to offer sacrifices day after day, first for his own sins, and then for the sins of the people. He sacrificed for their sins once for all when he offered himself. For the law appoints as high priests men who are weak; but the oath, which came after the law, appointed the Son, who has been made perfect forever. - Dedication

**Hebrews 12:9** - "Moreover, we have all had human fathers who disciplined us and we respected them for it. How much more should we submit to the Father of our spirits and live!" - Fatherhood

**Hebrews 13** - "So we say with confidence, "The Lord is my helper; I will not be afraid. What can man do to me?"-Fear

**James 1:12-13** - Blessed is the man who perseveres under trial, because when he has stood the test, he will receive the crown of life that God has promised to those who love him. When tempted, no one should say, "God is tempting me." For God cannot be tempted by evil, nor does he tempt anyone - Intro

**James 1:19-20-** "My dear brothers, take note of this: Everyone should be quick to listen, slow to speak and slow to become angry, for man's anger does not bring about the righteous life that God desires" – Listening

**James 1:19-27** - But whoever catches a glimpse of the revealed counsel of God—the free life!—Even out of the corner of his eye, and sticks with it, is no distracted scatterbrain but a man or woman of action. That person will find delight and affirmation in the action. - Signs

**James 1:27** - "Religion that God our Father accepts as pure and faultless is this: to look after orphans and widows in their distress and to keep oneself from being polluted by the world. "- Follow, Balance

**James 4:13-15**- "Now listen, you who say, "Today or tomorrow we will go to this or that city, spend a year there, carry on business and make money." Why, you do not even know what will happen tomorrow. What is your life? You are a mist that appears for a little while and then vanishes. Instead, you ought to say, "If it is the Lord's will, we will live and do this or that." Goals

**Romans 1:16** - I am not ashamed of the gospel, because it is the power of God for the salvation of everyone who believes: first for the Jew, then for the Gentile." – Revolution

**Romans 8:28** – "And we know that God causes all things to work together for good to those who love God, to those who are called according to His purpose." -Looking Forward, FIP

**Romans 11:29** - "For God's gifts and His call are irrevocable."- Talents

**Romans 12:1-2** - "Therefore, I urge you, brothers, in view of God's mercy, to offer your bodies as living sacrifices, holy and pleasing to God—this is your spiritual act of worship. Do not conform any longer to the pattern of this world, but be transformed by the renewing of your mind. Then you will be able to test and approve what God's will is—his good, pleasing and perfect will."-Success, Follow

**Romans 12:12** – "Be joyful in hope, patient in affliction, faithful in prayer."-FIP

**Romans13: 11** "And do this, understanding the present time. The hour has come for you to wake up from your slumber, because our salvation is nearer now than when we first believed."- Revolution

**Ephesians 4:22-24** - "You were taught, with regard to your former way of life, to put off your old self, which is being corrupted by its deceitful desires; to be made new in the attitude of your minds; and to put on the new self, created to be like God in true righteousness and holiness." - Prioritizing

**Ephesians 5:14** - "for the light makes everything visible. This is why it is said, "Awake, O sleeper, rise up from the dead, and Christ will give you light."- Revolution

**Ephesians 5:15-17**- "Be very careful, then, how you live--not as unwise but as wise, making the most of every opportunity, because the days are evil.  Therefore do not be foolish, but understand what the Lord's will is."-Looking Forward & Time

**Ephesians 5:23-33** - Love your wives, just as Christ loved the church and gave himself up for her to make her holy, cleansing her by the washing with water through the word, and to present her to himself as a radiant church, without stain or wrinkle or any other blemish, but holy and blameless. In this same way, husbands ought to love their wives as their own bodies. He who loves his wife loves himself. After all, no one ever hated his own body, but he feeds and cares for it, just as Christ does the church — for we are members of his body. "For this reason a man will leave his father and mother and be united to his wife, and the two will become one flesh." [This is a profound mystery — but I am talking about Christ and the church. However, each one of you also must love his wife as he loves himself, and the wife must respect her husband. – Intro

**Ephesians 5:25-33** -Husbands, love your wives, just as Christ loved the church and gave himself up for her to make her holy, cleansing her by the washing with water through the word, and to present her to himself as a radiant church, without stain or wrinkle or any other blemish, but holy and blameless. In this same way, husbands ought to love their wives as their own bodies. He who loves his wife loves himself. After all, no one ever hated his own body, but he feeds and cares for it, just as Christ does the church for we are members of his body." For this reason a man will leave his father and mother and be united to his wife, and the two will become one flesh." This is a profound mystery-but I am talking about Christ and the church. However, each one of you also must love his wife as he loves himself. - Intro

**Ephesians 5:28-30** - In the same way, husbands ought to love their wives as they love their own bodies. For a man is actually loving himself when he loves his wife. No one hates his own body but lovingly cares for it, just as Christ cares for his body, which is the church and we are his body. -Intro

**Ephesians 6:4** - "Fathers, do not exasperate your children; instead, bring them up in the training and instruction of the Lord." - Fatherhood

**Philippians 2:5-8** -"Your attitude should be the same as that of Christ Jesus: Who, being in very nature God, did not consider equality with God something to be grasped, but made himself nothing, taking the very nature of a servant, being made in human likeness. And being found in appearance as a man, he humbled himself and became obedient to death- even death on a cross!"-Follow

Len Stubbs

**Philippians 2:6-8** - "Your attitude should be the same as that of Christ Jesus: Who, being in very nature God, did not consider equality with God something to be grasped, but made Himself nothing, taking the very nature of a servant, being made in human likeness. And being found in appearance as a man, He humbled Himself and became obedient to death— even death on a cross!"-POF

**Philippians 2:14-16** – "Do all things without grumbling or questioning, that you may be blameless and innocent, children of God without blemish in the midst of a crooked and twisted generation, among whom you shine as lights in the world, holding fast to the word of life, so that in the day of Christ I may be proud that I did not run in vain or labor in vain". -Looking Forward

**Philippians 3:13-14** - "Brothers, I do not consider myself yet to have taken hold of it. But one thing I do: Forgetting what is behind and straining toward what is ahead, I press on toward the goal to win the prize for which God has called me heavenward in Christ Jesus." Follow

**Philippians 3:13** - No, dear brothers and sisters, I have not yet achieved it, but I focus on this one thing: Forgetting the past and looking forward to what lies ahead. - Looking Forward

**Colossians 1:16** - "For by him all things were created: things in heaven and on earth, visible and invisible, whether thrones or powers or rulers or authorities; all things were created by him and for him. – Prioritizing

**Colossians 3:2 -** "Fathers, do not embitter your children, or they will become discouraged." - Fatherhood

**Colossians 3:9-10** - "Do not lie to each other, since you have taken off your old self with its practices and have put on the new self, which is being renewed in knowledge in the image of its Creator." – Prioritizing

**Colossians - 3:19** - Husbands, love your wives and do not be harsh with them- Intro

**Colossians 3:21** - Fathers, do not embitter your children, or they will become discouraged. - Intro

**Galatians 3:8 -** There is neither Jew nor Greek, slave nor free, male nor female, for you are all one in Christ Jesus. Intro

**Timothy 4:14 -** "Do not neglect the gift that is in you, which was given to you by prophecy with the laying on of the hands of the eldership." – Skills

**1 Timothy 3:4 -** "He must manage his own family well and see that his children obey him with proper respect." – Fatherhood

**1 Timothy 3:2-7,12 -** Now the overseer must be above reproach, the husband of but one wife, temperate, self-controlled, respectable, hospitable, able to teach, not given to drunkenness, not violent but gentle, not quarrelsome, not a lover of money. He must manage his own family well and see that his children obey him with proper respect. If anyone does not know how to manage his own family, how can he take care of God's church? He must not be a recent convert, or he may become conceited and fall under the same judgment as the devil. He must also have a good reputation with outsiders, so that he will not fall into disgrace and into the devil's trap. A deacon must be the husband of but one wife and must manage his children and his household well. -Intro

**1 Timothy 5:1-3 -** Treat younger men as brothers, older women as mothers, and younger women as sisters, with absolute purity. Give proper recognition to those widows who are really in need. -Intro

**1 Timothy 5:8** - "If anyone does not provide for his relatives, and especially for his immediate family, he has denied the faith and is worse than an unbeliever." – Fatherhood

**1 TIMOTHY 5:17** - "The elders who direct the affairs of the church well are worthy of double honor, especially those whose work is preaching and teaching." – Leadership

**2 Timothy 1:6** - "Therefore I remind you to stir up the gift of God which is in you through the laying on of my hands." –Talents

**2 Timothy 1:7** - "For God has not given us a spirit of fear, but of power and of love and of a sound mind." -Fear

**2 TIMOTHY 3:16-17** – "All Scripture is God-breathed and is useful for teaching, rebuking, correcting and training in righteousness, so that the man of God may be thoroughly equipped for every good work." – Balance, Leadership

**2 Timothy 4:2** - "Preach the word; be ready in season and out of season; reprove, rebuke, exhort, with great patience and instruction."- Revolution

**TITUS 1:9** - "He must hold firmly to the trustworthy message as it has been taught, so that he can encourage others by sound doctrine and refute those who oppose it." - Leadership

**Titus 2:2** - Teach the older men to be temperate, worthy of respect, self-controlled, and sound in faith, in love and endurance. - Intro

**Titus 2: 6-7** - Similarly, encourage the young men to be self-controlled. In everything set them an example by doing what is good. In your teaching show integrity, seriousness. - Intro

**Titus 2:2-8** - Teach the older men to be temperate, worthy of respect, self-controlled, and sound in faith, in love and in endurance. Likewise, teach the older women to be reverent in the way they live, not to be slanderers or addicted too much wine, but to teach what is good. Then they can train the younger women to love their husbands and children, to be self-controlled and pure, to be busy at home, to be kind, and to be subject to their husbands, so that no one will malign the word of God. Similarly, encourage the young men to be self-controlled. In everything set them an example by doing what is good. In your teaching show integrity, seriousness and soundness of speech that cannot be condemned, so that those who oppose you may be ashamed because they have nothing bad to say about us. - Intro

**Titus 2:11-12-** "or the grace of God that bring salvation hath appeared to all men, Teaching us that, denying ungodliness and worldly lusts, we should live soberly, righteously, and godly, in this present world" – Prioritize

**1 Thessalonians 5:4-5** – "But you, brothers, are not in darkness so that this day should surprise you like a thief. You are all sons of the light and sons of the day. We do not belong to the night or to the darkness." – Revolution

**1 Peter 3:7** - Husbands, in the same way be considerate as you live with your wives, and treat them with respect as the weaker partner and as heirs with you of the gracious gift of life, so that nothing will hinder your prayers. - Intro

**1 PETER 5:3** – "not lording it over those entrusted to you, but being examples to the flock." - Leadership

**Revelation 4:11** - "You are worthy, our Lord and God to receive glory and honor and power, for you created all things, and by your will they were created and have their being." - Prioritizing

**Philippians 2:6-8** - *"Your attitude should be the same as that of Christ Jesus: Who, being in very nature God, did not consider equality with God something to be grasped, but made Himself nothing, taking the very nature of a servant, being made in human likeness. And being found in appearance as a man, He humbled Himself and became obedient to death— even death on a cross!"*

# CHAPTER NINETEEN

## APPENDIX

**Here is some of what the Lord has to say about His expectations of Men in His word.**

**Advice to Men & Husbands:**

1) **In Psalm 103:13** - As a father has compassion on his children, so the LORD has compassion on those who fear him;

2) **In Proverbs 6:20-22-** My son, keep your father's commands and do not forsake your mother's teaching. Bind them upon your heart forever; fasten them around your neck. When you walk, they will guide you; when you sleep, they will speak to you.

3) **In Proverbs 7:1-5** - My son, keep my words and store up my commands within you. Keep my commands and you will live; guard my teachings as the apple of your eye. Bind them on your fingers; write them on the tablet of your heart. Say to wisdom, "You are my sister," and call understanding your kinsman; they will keep you from the adulteress, from the wayward wife with her seductive words.

4) **In Proverbs 3:13-18** - Blessed is the man who finds wisdom, the man who gains understanding, for she is more profitable than silver and yields better returns than gold. She is more precious than rubies; nothing you desire can compare with her. Long life is in her right hand; in her left hand are riches and honor. Her ways are pleasant ways, and all her paths are peace. She is a tree of life to those who embrace her; those who lay hold of her will be blessed.

5) **In Proverbs 10:9** - The man of integrity walks securely, but he who takes crooked paths will be found out.

6) **In Proverbs - 20:7-** The righteous man leads a blameless life; blessed are his children after him.

7) **In Proverbs 28:6** - Better a poor man whose walk is blameless than a rich man whose ways are perverse.

8) **In Proverbs 29:23** - A man's pride brings him low, but a man of lowly spirit gains honor.

9) **In Corinthians 7:34** - But a married man is concerned about the affairs of this world how he can please his wife— and his interests are divided. An unmarried woman or virgin is concerned about the Lord's affairs: Her aim is to be devoted to the Lord in both body and spirit.

But a married woman is concerned about the affairs of this world how she can please her husband. I am saying this for your own good, not to restrict you, but that you may live in a right way in undivided devotion to the Lord.

10) **In 1 Corinthians 11:3 -** "But I want you to know that the head of every man is Christ, the head of woman is man, and the head of Christ is God"

11) **In 1 Corinthians 11:8-9,11-12 -** For man did not come from woman, but woman from man; neither was man created for woman, but woman for man. In the Lord, however, woman is not independent of man, nor is man independent of woman. For as woman came from man, so also man is born of woman. But everything comes from God.

12) **In Ephesians 5:23-33 -** Love your wives, just as Christ loved the church and gave himself up for her to make her holy, cleansing her by the washing with water through the word, and to present her to himself as a radiant church, without stain or wrinkle or any other blemish, but holy and blameless. In this same way, husbands ought to love their wives as their own bodies. He who loves his wife loves himself. After all, no one ever hated his own body, but he feeds and cares for it, just as Christ does the church for we are members of his body. "For this reason a man will leave his father and mother and be united to his wife, and the two will become one flesh." This is a profound mystery but I am talking about Christ and the church. However, each one of you also must love his wife as he loves himself, and the wife must respect her husband.

13) **In 1 Timothy 3:2-7,12 -** Now the overseer must be above reproach, the husband of but one wife, temperate, self-controlled, respectable, hospitable, able to teach, not given to drunkenness, not violent but gentle, not quarrelsome, not a lover of money. He must manage his own family well and see that his children obey him with proper respect. If anyone does not know how to manage his own family,

how can he take care of God's church? He must not be a recent convert, or he may become conceited and fall under the same judgment as the devil. He must also have a good reputation with outsiders, so that he will not fall into disgrace and into the devil's trap. A deacon must be the husband of but one wife and must manage his children and his household well.

14) **In 1 Timothy 5:8** - If anyone does not provide for his relatives, and especially for his immediate family, he has denied the faith and is worse than an unbeliever.

15) **In James 1:12-13** - Blessed is the man who perseveres under trial, because when he has stood the test, he will receive the crown of life that God has promised to those who love him. When tempted, no one should say, "God is tempting me." For God cannot be tempted by evil, nor does he tempt anyone

15) **In Titus 2:2-8** - Teach the older men to be temperate, worthy of respect, self-controlled, and sound in faith, in love and in endurance. Likewise, teach the older women to be reverent in the way they live, not to be slanderers or addicted too much wine, but to teach what is good. Then they can train the younger women to love their husbands and children, to be self-controlled and pure, to be busy at home, to be kind, and to be subject to their husbands, so that no one will malign the word of God. Similarly, encourage the young men to be self-controlled. In everything set them an example by doing what is good. In your teaching show integrity, seriousness and soundness of speech that cannot be condemned, so that those who oppose you may be ashamed because they have nothing bad to say about us.

16) **In 1 Peter 3:7** - Husbands, in the same way be considerate as you live with your wives, and treat them with respect as

the weaker partner and as heirs with you of the gracious gift of life, so that nothing will hinder your prayers.

**Faithful Men:**

1) **In Proverbs 17:27** - A man of knowledge uses words with restraint, and a man of understanding is even-tempered.

2) **In Proverbs 20:6-** Many a man claims to have unfailing love, but a faithful man who can find?

3) **In Matthew 26:41** - Watch and pray so that you will not fall into temptation. The spirit is willing, but the body is weak.

4) **In Luke 16:10** - Whoever can be trusted with very little can also be trusted with much, and whoever is dishonest with very little will also be dishonest with much.

5) **In 1 Corinthians 10:13** - No temptation has seized you except what is common to man. And God is faithful; he will not let you be tempted beyond what you can bear. But when you are tempted, he will also provide a way out so that you can stand up under it.

6) **In Galatians 3:8** - There is neither Jew nor Greek, slave nor free, male nor female, for you are all one in Christ Jesus.

7) **In Colossians 3:19** - Many a man claims to have unfailing love, but a faithful man who can find?

**Husbands Love Your Wives:**

1) **In Genesis 24:67** - Isaac brought her into the tent of his mother Sarah, and he married Rebekah. So she became his wife, and he loved her; and Isaac was comforted after his mother's death.

2) **In Genesis 29:10-11** -When Jacob saw Rachel daughter of Laban, his mother's brother, and Laban's sheep, he went over and rolled the stone away from the mouth of the well and watered his uncle's sheep. Then Jacob kissed Rachel and began to weep aloud.

3) **In Genesis 29:18-20** -Jacob was in love with Rachel and said, "I'll work for you seven years in return for your younger daughter Rachel." Laban said, "It's better that I give her to you than to some other man. Stay here with me." So Jacob served seven years to get Rachel, but they seemed like only a few days to him because of his love for her.

4) **In Ephesians 5:25-33** -Husbands, love your wives, just as Christ loved the church and gave himself up for her to make her holy, cleansing her by the washing with water through the word, and to present her to himself as a radiant church, without stain or wrinkle or any other blemish, but holy and blameless. In this same way, husbands ought to love their wives as their own bodies. He who loves his wife loves himself. After all, no one ever hated his own body, but he feeds and cares for it, just as Christ does the church for we are members of his body." For this reason a man will leave his father and mother and be united to his wife, and the two will become one flesh." This is a profound mystery-but I am talking about Christ and the church. However, each one of you also must love his wife as he loves himself...

5) **In Colossians - 3:19** - Husbands, love your wives and do not be harsh with them

## Responsibility of Men in Marriage:

1) **In 1 Timothy 5:8** - If anyone does not provide for his relatives, and especially for his immediate family, he has denied the faith and is worse than an unbeliever.

2) **In Colossians 3:19** - You husbands must love your wives and never treat them harshly.

## Men of Character:

1) **In 1 Samuel 16:7** - But the Lord said to Samuel, "Do not consider his appearance or his height, for I have rejected him. The Lord does not look at the things man looks at. Man looks at the outward appearance, but the Lord looks at the heart.

2) **In Daniel 1:8** - But Daniel resolved not to defile himself...

3) **In John 7:24** - Stop judging by mere appearances, and make a right judgment.

## Praiseworthy Men:

1) **In 1 Chronicles 28:9** - And you, my son Solomon, acknowledge the God of your father, and serve him with wholehearted devotion and with a willing mind, for the Lord searches every heart and understands every motive behind the thoughts. If you seek him, he will be found by you; but if you forsake him, he will reject you forever.

2) **In Psalm 15:2-5** -He whose walk is blameless and who does what is righteous, who speaks the truth from his heart And has no slander on tongue, who does his neighbor no wrong and casts no slur on his fellow man, Who despises a vile man but honors those who fear the Lord, who keeps his oath even when it hurts, Who lends his money without

usury and does not accept a bribe against the innocent. He who does these things will never be shaken.

3) **In Psalm 128:1-4** - Blessed are all who fear the Lord, who walk in his ways. You will eat the fruit of your labor; blessings and prosperity will be yours. Your wife will be like a fruitful vine within your house; your sons will be like olive shoots around your table. Thus is the man blessed who fears the Lord.

4) **In Titus 2:2, 6-7** - Teach the older men to be temperate, worthy of respect, self-controlled, and sound in faith, in love and endurance. Similarly, encourage the young men to be self-controlled. In everything set them an example by doing what is good. In your teaching show integrity, seriousness.

**Behavior of Men with Women:**

1) **In Matthew 7:12** -- In everything, do to others what you would have them do to you

2) **In Luke 6:31** - Do to others, as you would have them do to you.

3) **In 1 Timothy 5:1-3** -Treat younger men as brothers, older women as mothers, and younger women as sisters, with absolute purity. Give proper recognition to those widows who are really in need.

4) **In Ephesians 5:28-30** - In the same way, husbands ought to love their wives as they love their own bodies. For a man is actually loving himself when he loves his wife. No one hates his own body but lovingly cares for it, just as Christ cares for his body, which is the church and we are his body.

## Fathers:

1) **In Malachi 4:6** - He will turn the hearts of the fathers to their children, and the hearts of the children to their fathers; or else I will come and strike the land with a curse.

2) **In Colossians 3:21** - Fathers, do not embitter your children, or they will become discouraged.

3) **In Ephesians 6:4** - Fathers, do not exasperate your children; instead, bring them up in the training and instruction of the Lord.

**1 Corinthians 9:19-23-** *Though I am free and belong to no man, I make myself a slave to everyone, to win as many as possible. To the Jews I became like a Jew, to win the Jews. To those under the law I became like one under the law (though I myself am not under the law), so as to win those under the law. To those not having the law I became like one not having the law (though I am not free from God's law but am under Christ's law), so as to win those not having the law. To the weak I became weak, to win the weak. I have become all things to all men so that by all possible means I might save some. I do all this for the sake of the gospel that I may share in its blessings.*

# CHAPTER TWENTY

## WHO ARE YOU EXERCISE

**Most Meaningful Bible Passages (this week)**

**Most Important people in my life: (Forever)**

Len Stubbs

## **Single most important focus in my life:**


## **Bio stuff:**


## **Business:**


## **Entrepreneur:**


## **Current Career:**


## **Future Desire:**


## **Athletically:**


## **Greatest Achievement:**

**What you most likely don't know about me:**

**Greatest Strength's:**

**Greatest Weakness:**

**Greatest Strength from wife/husband's vantage point:**

**Greatest weakness from wife/husband's vantage point:**

**My addiction:**

**Life impacting events:**

**Most meaningful non-biblical quote:**

**Tombstone:**

Len Stubbs

## **Most serene moment in Church:**